The Standard for English Grammar Books

# GRAMMAR ZONE
# WORKBOOK

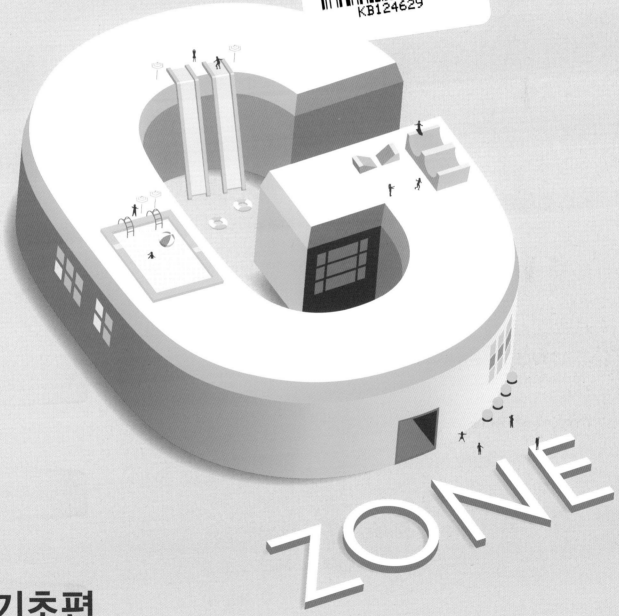

ZONE

기초편

# GRAMMAR ZONE
# WORKBOOK 기초편

| | |
|---|---|
| **지은이** | NE능률 영어교육연구소 |
| **선임연구원** | 한정은 |
| **연구원** | 박진향 정희은 이은비 이경란 강혜진 |
| **영문교열** | Benjamin Robinson  Patrick Ferraro |
| **표지 · 내지디자인** | 닷츠 |
| **내지일러스트** | 이상경 김기환 |
| **맥편집** | 이인선 |
| **영업** | 한기영, 이경구, 박인규, 정철교, 김남준, 이우현 |
| **마케팅** | 박혜선, 남경진, 이지원, 김여진 |
| **원고에 도움을 주신 분** | 구희진 |

# NE능률이
# 미래를
# 창조합니다.

건강한 배움의 고객가치를 제공하겠다는 꿈을 실현하기 위해
40년이 넘는 시간 동안 열심히 달려왔습니다.

앞으로도 끊임없는 연구와 노력을 통해
당연한 것을 멈추지 않고

고객, 기업, 직원 모두가 함께 성장하는 NE능률이 되겠습니다.

NE 능률

# Practice is the best of all instructions.

연습은 가장 좋은 가르침이다.

---

유명한 운동 선수, 최고의 과학자, 노벨상을 받은 작가, 그 누구도 자신들이 이루어낸 것이 하루 아침에 완성되었다고 말하는 사람은 없습니다. 그들을 성공으로 이끈 것은 무엇일까요? 여러분도 알다시피 목표를 달성하고 꿈을 이루는 데 성실하게 연습하는 것만큼 효과적인 무기는 없습니다. 저희는 여러분을 '문법 지존(至尊)'의 세계로 인도할 수 있는 가장 좋은 무기를 준비하였습니다. G-ZONE에서 학습한 모든 것을 이 WORKBOOK을 통해 연습하여 여러분 모두 문법의 '지존'이 되길 바랍니다. 꾸준한 연습을 다짐하는 여러분을 응원합니다.

# 구성과 특징

## 진단 TEST

현재 자신이 알고 있는 문법 항목과 모르는 문법 항목을 점검할 수 있게 하는 TEST입니다. Workbook을 본격적으로 공부하기 전에 진단 TEST부터 풀어 보고, 자신이 부족한 부분이 어디인지 파악한 후 학습 계획을 세워봅시다. 각 문제 옆에는 연관된 Grammar Zone 본 교재의 UNIT이 표기되어 있으니, 틀린 문제에 해당하는 UNIT을 본 교재로 먼저 복습하면 효율적인 학습이 가능합니다.

## TEST

각 UNIT을 제대로 학습하였는지 확인할 수 있는 다양한 유형의 문제를 수록하였습니다. 비교적 간단한 드릴형 문제에서부터 사고력과 응용력을 요하는 문제까지 꼼꼼히 풀어본 후 부족한 부분에 대해 추가 학습 계획을 세워 봅시다.

## CHECK UP

각 UNIT의 핵심 문법을 간단한 문제를 통해 확인할 수 있습니다. 각 문제 옆에는 해당 문법을 다룬 본 교재의 항목이 표시되어 있으므로, 추가 학습이 필요하다면 해당 항목을 복습한 후 Workbook으로 돌아오세요.

## WRITING PRACTICE

쓰기 연습이 가능한 문제를 충분히 제시하였습니다. 수행평가나 서술형 문제 대비가 가능하며 궁극적으로 영어 쓰기 실력을 향상시켜 줍니다.

## 실전 TEST

여러 UNIT의 문법 사항을 종합적으로 확인할 수 있도록 총 6회의 실전 TEST를 제공합니다. 중간고사 및 기말고사에 대비할 수 있도록 문제 유형과 난이도 등을 실제에 맞추어 구성하였으며, 실제 기출을 응용한 주관식 문제를 제시하여 수행평가 및 서술형 문제 대비에도 유용합니다.

# Contents

# Study Tracker

그래머존 본책의 학습일을 기입한 후, 워크북으로 확인 학습한 날짜도 함께 적어 봅시다. 워크북까지 학습을 끝낸 후 나의 '문법 이해도'를 점검해 봅시다.

| 본책<br>목차 / 학습일 | | | | | 워크북<br>UNIT / 학습일 | | | | | | | | | 문법 이해도 | | |
|---|---|---|---|---|---|---|---|---|---|---|---|---|---|---|---|---|
| | | | | | 진단 TEST | | | | | | 월 | 일 | | 상 | 중 | 하 |
| Part 1 | 월 | 일 ~ | 월 | 일 | 01 월 일 | 02 | 월 | 일 | 03 | 월 | 일 | | | 상 | 중 | 하 |
| | | | | | 04 월 일 | 05 | 월 | 일 | 06 | 월 | 일 | | | | | |
| | | | | | 07 월 일 | 08 | 월 | 일 | 09 | 월 | 일 | | | | | |
| | | | | | 10 월 일 | | | | | | | | | | | |
| | | | | | 실전 TEST 01 | | | | | | 월 | 일 | | 상 | 중 | 하 |
| 시제 | 월 | 일 ~ | 월 | 일 | 11 월 일 | 12 | 월 | 일 | 13 | 월 | 일 | | | 상 | 중 | 하 |
| | | | | | 14 월 일 | 15 | 월 | 일 | | | | | | | | |
| 조동사 | 월 | 일 ~ | 월 | 일 | 16 월 일 | 17 | 월 | 일 | 18 | 월 | 일 | | | 상 | 중 | 하 |
| | | | | | 19 월 일 | | | | | | | | | | | |
| 수동태 | 월 | 일 ~ | 월 | 일 | 20 월 일 | 21 | 월 | 일 | | | | | | 상 | 중 | 하 |
| | | | | | 실전 TEST 02 | | | | | | 월 | 일 | | 상 | 중 | 하 |
| 명사 · 관사 | 월 | 일 ~ | 월 | 일 | 22 월 일 | 23 | 월 | 일 | | | | | | 상 | 중 | 하 |
| 대명사 | 월 | 일 ~ | 월 | 일 | 24 월 일 | 25 | 월 | 일 | 26 | 월 | 일 | | | 상 | 중 | 하 |
| 형용사 · 부사 | 월 | 일 ~ | 월 | 일 | 27 월 일 | 28 | 월 | 일 | 29 | 월 | 일 | | | 상 | 중 | 하 |
| | | | | | 30 월 일 | | | | | | | | | | | |
| 전치사 | 월 | 일 ~ | 월 | 일 | 31 월 일 | 32 | 월 | 일 | 33 | 월 | 일 | | | 상 | 중 | 하 |
| | | | | | 실전 TEST 03 | | | | | | 월 | 일 | | 상 | 중 | 하 |
| 부정사 | 월 | 일 ~ | 월 | 일 | 34 월 일 | 35 | 월 | 일 | 36 | 월 | 일 | | | 상 | 중 | 하 |
| | | | | | 37 월 일 | | | | | | | | | | | |
| 동명사 | 월 | 일 ~ | 월 | 일 | 38 월 일 | 39 | 월 | 일 | 40 | 월 | 일 | | | 상 | 중 | 하 |
| 분사 | 월 | 일 ~ | 월 | 일 | 41 월 일 | 42 | 월 | 일 | 43 | 월 | 일 | | | 상 | 중 | 하 |
| | | | | | 실전 TEST 04 | | | | | | 월 | 일 | | 상 | 중 | 하 |
| 관계사 | 월 | 일 ~ | 월 | 일 | 44 월 일 | 45 | 월 | 일 | 46 | 월 | 일 | | | 상 | 중 | 하 |
| | | | | | 47 월 일 | | | | | | | | | | | |
| 접속사 | 월 | 일 ~ | 월 | 일 | 48 월 일 | 49 | 월 | 일 | 50 | 월 | 일 | | | 상 | 중 | 하 |
| | | | | | 실전 TEST 05 | | | | | | 월 | 일 | | 상 | 중 | 하 |
| 가정법 | 월 | 일 ~ | 월 | 일 | 51 월 일 | 52 | 월 | 일 | | | | | | 상 | 중 | 하 |
| 일치 · 화법 | 월 | 일 ~ | 월 | 일 | 53 월 일 | 54 | 월 | 일 | 55 | 월 | 일 | | | 상 | 중 | 하 |
| | | | | | 실전 TEST 06 | | | | | | 월 | 일 | | 상 | 중 | 하 |

# 진단 TEST

**UNIT 1** **1** Your car _____ very clean.
① a ② are ③ is ④ has

**UNIT 2, 11** **2** My parents _____ the 9 o'clock news these days.
① watch ② watchs ③ watches ④ watched

**UNIT 3, 11** **3** Jihyun _____ to middle school in the US last year, but now she is in Korea.
① go ② goes ③ goed ④ went

**UNIT 4** **4** Cows _____ meat.
① don't eat ② doesn't eat ③ doesn't eats ④ not eats

**UNIT 5** **5** A: Don't you like Maroon 5? B: _____.
① Yes, I don't ② No, I do ③ Yes, I do ④ No, you don't

**UNIT 10, 2** **6** James is not a big man, but he _____.
① look strong ② look strongly ③ looks strong ④ looks strongly

**UNIT 12** **7** She will be delighted if you _____.
① come ② will come ③ comes ④ coming

★ **UNIT 13** **8** I really wanted a smartphone and I _____ one.
① finally got ② finally have ③ have finally got ④ am finally having

**UNIT 14** **9** Bob isn't here now. He _____ Spain.
① has gone ② has gone to ③ has been to ④ has been for

**UNIT 14, 6** **10** A: I've seen Suzy before. B: Really? When _____ her?
① have you seen ② you have seen ③ did you see ④ you saw

**UNIT 16** **11** Maybe one day she _____ sing like Adele.
① will can ② can will ③ will be going to ④ will be able to

★ **UNIT 17** **12** _____ I borrow your bike for a day or two?
① May ② Can ③ Could ④ Will

**UNIT 19** **13** I have an upset stomach. I _____ have eaten so fast.
① can't ② must not ③ shouldn't ④ may not

**UNIT 20** **14** More and more Korean dramas _____ worldwide.
① watched ② is watched ③ are watching ④ are being watched

**UNIT 21** **15** Usually, textbooks _____ students in February.
① give ② are given ③ are given to ④ given to

**UNIT 22** **16** I was thirsty, so I drank five _____.
① water ② waters ③ glass of water ④ glasses of water

**UNIT 23** **17** After school, Ben usually plays _____ basketball with his friends.
① a ② an ③ the ④ (관사 없음)

**UNIT 27, 55** **18** There's _____ chance that you'll win the lottery. Don't buy a ticket.
① little ② a little ③ few ④ a few

**UNIT 32, 15** **19** He's been fixing the TV _____ more than four hours.
① since ② until ③ for ④ during

**UNIT 34** **20** Tell me _____ the answer.
① find where ② to where find ③ where to find ④ to find where

★ **UNIT 35** **21** She saved money _____ buy luxurious cosmetics.
① to ② for ③ in order to ④ so as to

**UNIT 36** **22** It was foolish _____ him to miss such a good opportunity.
① for ② of ③ to ④ with

**UNIT 39** **23** Please don't forget _____ me when you get home.
① call ② calling ③ to call ④ to calling

**UNIT 42** **24** I was very _____ with myself.
① disappoint ② disappoints ③ disappointing ④ disappointed

**UNIT 45** **25** _____ he really wants to do is to play the game himself.
① What ② That ③ Which ④ It

**UNIT 46** **26** I know a nice restaurant _____ the food is good and very cheap.
① that ② where ③ what ④ which

**UNIT 49, 12** **27** I don't know if Jack _____ us or not.
① join ② joins ③ will join ④ will joins

**UNIT 51** **28** If I _____ you, I would forgive him.
① am ② are ③ is ④ were

**UNIT 53** **29** A number of _____ going to participate in the tournament.
① athlete is ② athlete are ③ athletes is ④ athletes are

**UNIT 55** **30** A: I don't like his songs.　　B: _____. He sings badly.
① Neither do I ② Neither am I ③ So do I ④ So am I

# UNIT 01 be동사의 쓰임과 형태 변화

## ☑ CHECK UP  괄호 안에서 알맞은 것을 고르세요.

**1** I (am / is) a middle school student.　　　　　`B`

**2** You (are / is) my close friend.　　　　　`B`

**3** (We / It) are in the same class.　　　　　`B`

**4** (She / They) is a science teacher.　　　　　`B`

**5** Their books (are / is) under the chair.　　　　　`B`

## A  [보기]에서 알맞은 말을 골라 빈칸을 채우세요.

[보기]　am　　are　　is

**1** Stephen King _____ a good writer.

**2** My friend _____ absent from school today.

**3** I _____ a NASA scientist.

**4** You _____ so lucky.

**5** The sky _____ clear and bright.

**6** She and I _____ classmates.

## B  예시와 같이 밑줄 친 부분을 줄여 쓰세요.

**0** They are old friends.　　　→　They're

**1** I am happy now.　　　→　_____

**2** He is a chef.　　　→　_____

**3** It is on the table.　　　→　_____

**4** You are so cool.　　　→　_____

**5** We are all from Africa.　　　→　_____

**6** She is at home with her mother.　　　→　_____

**C** 밑줄 친 be동사의 뜻이 '~이다, ~하다'이면 a를 쓰고, '~에 있다'이면 b를 쓰세요.

**1** He <u>is</u> a professor. _____

**2** Julia <u>is</u> in the cafe. _____

**3** They <u>are</u> American. _____

**4** Your cell phone <u>is</u> under the sofa. _____

**5** She <u>is</u> very angry. _____


**D** ⓐ와 ⓑ 중에서 어법상 옳지 <u>않은</u> 것을 골라 바르게 고쳐 쓰세요.

**1** My parents ⓐ <u>are</u> in Oxford. Their office ⓑ <u>are</u> on Green Street. _____

**2** You ⓐ <u>are</u> beautiful. That dress ⓑ <u>are</u> perfect. _____

**3** The tree ⓐ <u>is</u> really tall. ⓑ <u>Its</u> about 100 years old. _____

**4** These shoes ⓐ <u>are</u> too tight. ⓑ <u>It are</u> dirty, too. _____

**5** This ⓐ <u>is</u> his first year in college. His major ⓑ <u>are</u> physics. _____


## WRITING PRACTICE

우리말과 일치하도록 각 상자 속 어구를 하나씩 연결하여 문장을 완성하세요.

| Her name | are | 170 cm tall |
| The history books | are | Kim Somi |
| I | is | on the desk |
| Ronaldo and Messi | am | great soccer players |

**1** 그녀의 이름은 김소미이다. → _____.

**2** 호날두와 메시는 훌륭한 축구선수이다. → _____.

**3** 나는 키가 170cm이다. → _____.

**4** 그 역사책들은 책상 위에 있다. → _____.

# UNIT 02 일반동사의 현재형

## CHECK UP

**괄호 안에서 알맞은 것을 고르세요.**

**1** He (eat / eats) breakfast every day.　　　　　　　B

**2** Jessica (begin / begins) her work at 9:00.　　　　B

**3** (He / They) often plays tennis.　　　　　　　　　B

**4** Cindy (gos / goes) to school at 8 o'clock.　　　　C

**5** My son (studys / studies) English for two hours every day.　　C

## A

**예시와 같이 밑줄 친 말을 대명사로 바꾸어 문장을 완성하세요.**

**0** Grace / wash her hands before every meal.

→ She washes her hands before every meal.

**1** The students / like their teacher.

→ _____ .

**2** Laura and I / work at a café together.

→ _____ .

**3** This house / have two bedrooms.

→ _____ .

**4** Mr. Kim / brush his teeth three times a day.

→ _____ .

## B

**괄호 안의 동사를 현재형으로 바꿔 빈칸을 완성하세요.**

**1** Judy _____ (have) a brother and two sisters.

**2** Minho _____ (go) to school by bus.

**3** Kelly _____ (like) Mexican food.

**4** Simon _____ (play) baseball on Sundays.

**5** A refrigerator _____ (keep) food cool.

**6** He _____ (do) the laundry on weekends.

**C**  빈칸에 take 또는 takes를 알맞게 쓰세요.

**1** Jina and Tom _____ a walk every morning. There is a beautiful park near their house. They always _____ their dog to the park.

**2** Jina works at a bank. She _____ the subway to work. It _____ about thirty minutes to get to the office.

**D**  밑줄 친 동사를 알맞은 현재형으로 바꿔 쓰세요. (바꿀 필요 없으면 × 표시할 것)

**1** The baby <u>cry</u> a lot.  _____

**2** The sisters <u>have</u> a cute dog.  _____

**3** My parents never <u>watch</u> TV.  _____

**4** He <u>worry</u> about his son.  _____

**5** The women <u>do</u> yoga with me in the morning.  _____

**6** John <u>enjoy</u> jogging every morning with his wife.  _____

## WRITING PRACTICE

우리말과 일치하도록 괄호 안의 말을 이용하여 문장을 완성하세요.

**1** 소진이는 서울에 산다. (live in)

Sojin _____ _____ _____ .

**2** Tyler는 3개국어를 한다. (speak, languages)

Tyler _____ _____ _____ .

**3** 그 귀여운 소녀는 방과 후에 피아노를 친다. (play the piano)

The cute little girl _____ _____ _____ after school.

**4** 내 남동생과 나는 매일 체육관에 간다. (go to the gym)

My brother and I _____ _____ _____ _____ every day.

# UNIT 03 be동사·일반동사의 과거형

☑ **CHECK UP** 괄호 안에서 알맞은 것을 고르세요.

**1** I (was / were) born in 2001.  `A`

**2** They (was / were) angry with me yesterday.  `A`

**3** Paul (plaied / played) baseball last Saturday.  `B-1`

**4** We (planed / planned) a surprise party for him.  `B-1`

**5** I (sended / sent) a letter to you last month.  `B-2`

## A  빈칸에 was 또는 were를 알맞게 쓰세요.

**1** Eddie _____ very sick last week.

**2** Miss Smith _____ in the office today.

**3** Those students _____ at the museum.

**4** He _____ my close friend at that time.

**5** My friends and I _____ at the concert last night.

**6** Andy _____ in France with his parents last year.

## B  [보기]에서 알맞은 말을 골라 빈칸을 채우세요.

[보기]  am   is   was   are   were

**1** Monica _____ in London in 2010.

**2** They _____ very tired last night.

**3** Mom, I _____ in Malaysia now.

**4** The school _____ closed yesterday.

**5** Ms. Jordan _____ my science teacher two years ago.

**6** We _____ really hungry now. What's for lunch?

**7** The shopping mall _____ very crowded now.

**C** 괄호 안의 동사를 과거형으로 바꿔 빈칸을 완성하세요.

**1** Olivia _____ (lose) her wallet yesterday.

**2** Victoria _____ (cook) dinner last night.

**3** I _____ (read) the book last week.

**4** Alex _____ (sing) a song at church this morning.

**5** Lucas and Sarah _____ (come) to Korea 10 years ago.

**6** Dan _____ (go) to hospital this morning.


**D** 밑줄 친 부분 중 어법상 옳은 것에 ○ 표시하고, 옳지 않은 것은 바르게 고쳐 쓰세요.

**1** The man give me this card last Valentine's Day.          _____

**2** I spended 500 dollars last month.          _____

**3** Last summer we go on a trip to Thailand.          _____

**4** My father bought a new car last year.          _____

**5** I speaked with Josh yesterday.          _____

**6** They took tennis lessons together for a year.          _____

**7** I put my USB on the table, and he threw it away by accident.          _____


## WRITING PRACTICE

우리말과 일치하도록 괄호 안의 동사를 이용하여 문장을 완성하세요.

**1** 그녀는 나에게 자기 이름을 말해주었다. (tell)

She _____ me _____ _____.

**2** 우리는 지난주에 코미디 영화를 보았다. (see)

We _____ a _____ _____ last week.

**3** Maria는 우리를 위해 특별한 케이크를 만들었다. (make)

Maria _____ a _____ _____ for us.

**4** 모차르트는 네 살 때 피아노를 치기 시작했다. (be, start)

When Mozart _____ four years old, he _____ to play the piano.

# UNIT 04 be동사·일반동사의 부정문

정답 및 해설 p.07

↗ **CHECK UP** 괄호 안에서 알맞은 것을 고르세요.

**1** Francisco (isn't / aren't) American.　　　　　　　`B`

**2** I (wasn't / weren't) there this morning.　　　　　`B`

**3** Those (isn't / aren't) my pencils.　　　　　　　`B`

**4** Sophia (did not / not did) write the book alone.　`C`

**5** He doesn't (has / have) a girlfriend.　　　　　　`C`

**A** [보기]에서 알맞은 말을 하나씩 골라 빈칸을 채우세요.

> [보기]　 am not　　 are not　　 is not　　 was not　　 were not

**1** You _____ short. You're tall enough.

**2** Chess _____ an easy game. It has many rules.

**3** The movie _____ exciting. It was a little boring.

**4** We _____ home last night. We were at a party.

**5** I _____ a boy anymore. I'm twenty years old.

**B** 밑줄 친 부분을 부정문으로 바꾸세요. (줄임말을 이용할 것)

**1** Allison likes spicy food. She likes sweet things.

　→ _____

**2** I have two sisters, but I have any brothers.

　→ _____

**3** Max enjoys his job. He thinks it's too difficult.

　→ _____

**4** My parents are very busy, so they spend much time with me.

　→ _____

**5** Emily goes to bed early. She usually studies late at night.

　→ _____

**14**　G-ZONE WORKBOOK

**C** 예시와 같이 괄호 안의 동사를 이용하여 첫 번째 빈칸에는 과거형을, 두 번째 빈칸에는 과거시제의 부정문을 쓰세요.

    **0** Cathy got up early, but Tina didn't get up until noon. (get)

    **1** Natalie _____ the truth, but I _____ until yesterday. (know)

    **2** Noah _____ all the questions, but Emma _____ any questions. (answer)

    **3** Jill _____ in the lake, but Carol _____ with him. (swim)

    **4** Rob _____ Lucy to the party, but Lynn _____ any of her friends. (invite)

**D** 밑줄 친 부분 중 어법상 옳은 것에 ○ 표시하고, 옳지 않은 것은 바르게 고쳐 쓰세요.

    **1** I'm a stranger. I amn't familiar with this place, either. _____

    **2** He didn't tells me his name. I still don't know it. _____

    **3** She don't eat raw fish. She dislikes it. _____

    **4** It isn't your fault. We're not disappointed in you. _____

    **5** They wasn't late for class, but they didn't do their homework. _____

## WRITING PRACTICE

우리말과 일치하도록 각 상자 속 어구를 하나씩 연결하여 문장을 완성하세요.

| We | don't | difficult at all |
| The homework | isn't | here right now |
| Mr. Jones | didn't | have money now |
| Brandon | wasn't | listen to my advice |

**1** 우리는 지금 돈이 없다.     → _____.

**2** 그 숙제는 전혀 어렵지 않았다.     → _____.

**3** Jones 씨는 내 조언을 듣지 않았다.     → _____.

**4** Brandon은 지금 여기에 없다.     → _____.

# UNIT 05 be동사·일반동사의 의문문

☑ **CHECK UP**    괄호 안에서 알맞은 것을 고르세요.

**1** (Was / Were) Stella ill yesterday?    A

**2** (Do / Are) you love her?    B

**3** (Do / Does) he speak English?    B

**4** Did Olivia (live / lived) in an apartment?    B

**5** A: Aren't you tired? B: Yes, (I am / I'm not).    C

**A**    빈칸에 Do 또는 Does를 알맞게 쓰세요.

**1** _____ you like to read?

**2** _____ the movie start at eight?

**3** _____ I look better?

**4** _____ Sue have a cell phone?

**5** _____ Matt and Frank like football?

**6** _____ we need to wait for her?

**B**    문장을 의문문으로 바꿔 쓰세요.

**1** She likes yellow.

→ _____

**2** Ann is a shy girl.

→ _____

**3** Jason was nervous before the interview.

→ _____

**4** Karen painted this picture.

→ _____

**5** They made this birthday cake.

→ _____

**6** You wrote a book in Chinese.

→ _____

**C**      예시와 같이 그림과 일치하도록 괄호 안의 말을 이용하여 긍정의문문과 그 대답을 완성하세요.

**0**

A : <u>Are they</u> bananas?
B : <u>No, they aren't.</u> (they, are)

**1**

A : _____ any money?
B : _____ . (you, have)

**2**

A : _____ a pig?
B : _____ . (it, is)

**3**

A : _____ much hair?
B : _____ . (he, have)

---

## WRITING PRACTICE

우리말과 일치하도록 괄호 안의 말을 이용하여 문장을 완성하세요.

**1** 이것은 네 코트가 아니니? (not, your coat)

_____ _____ _____ _____?

**2** 이 케이크 맛있어? (taste good)

_____ _____ _____ _____?

**3** 너는 그가 걱정되지 않니? (not, worry about)

_____ _____ _____ _____?

**4** 그는 어젯밤에 그 호텔에서 묵었나요? (stay in)

_____ _____ _____ _____ the hotel last night?

# UNIT 06 의문사가 있는 의문문

정답 및 해설 p.09

☑ CHECK UP  **괄호 안에서 알맞은 것을 고르세요.**

**1** (When / Where) are you from?  `B-1`

**2** (Why / Where) did you tell me about it?  `B-3`

**3** (How / What) much are these shoes?  `B-4`

**4** (Who's / Whose) camera is that?  `B-5`

**5** (Who's / What's) your name?  `B-6`

---

**A**  **예시와 같이 주어진 말을 이용하여 의문문을 완성하세요. (주어진 동사의 시제와 일치시킬 것)**

**0** When / they / arrived
→ When did they arrive?

**1** Where / you / live
→ _____

**2** How old / your grandfather / is
→ _____

**3** Why / you / became / a firefighter
→ _____

**4** What / you / talked about
→ _____

---

**B**  **그림을 보고 [보기]에서 알맞은 말을 골라 빈칸을 채우세요.**

[보기]   where   who   what   how

**1** _____ is this girl?

**2** _____ is she doing?

**3** _____ is she? Is she on the stage?

**4** _____ old is she? She looks very young.

**C**  질문과 대답을 바르게 짝지으세요.

**1** What does she do?  •
**2** Where is she now?  •
**3** Does she have a pet?  •
**4** Is she married?  •
**5** What are her hobbies?  •

• (a) She is in her office.
• (b) She likes to read and go fishing.
• (c) She's a lawyer.
• (d) No, she doesn't like animals.
• (e) Yes, she is. She has two kids.

**D**  문장의 밑줄 친 부분을 바르게 고쳐 쓰세요.

**1** Where is you work?  _____
**2** When you came home?  _____
**3** Who cell phone is this?  _____
**4** Why did she goes to the hospital?  _____
**5** Many how bedrooms does the house have?  _____

---

**WRITING PRACTICE**

우리말과 일치하도록 괄호 안의 말을 바르게 배열하여 문장을 완성하세요.

**1** 누가 내 펜을 가져갔니? (took, my, who, pen)

→ _____ ?

**2** 중간고사가 언제니? (the, when, midterm exams, are)

→ _____ ?

**3** 너는 어젯밤에 어디에 있었니? (were, last night, where, you)

→ _____ ?

**4** 너는 파란 것과 빨간 것 중에 어떤 것이 더 좋니? (prefer, the red one, which, or, you, the blue one, do)

→ _____ ?

↗ **CHECK UP** **괄호 안에서 알맞은 것을 고르세요.**

**1** Ashley doesn't like (he / him). `A-1`

**2** Did you enjoy (your / you're) trip? `A-2`

**3** This is my favorite shirt. I like (its / it's) pattern. `A-2`

**4** Is this umbrella (your / yours)? `A-2`

**5** He is the (childrens' / children's) father. `B-2`

**A** **우리말과 일치하도록 빈칸에 알맞은 대명사를 쓰세요.**

**1** 나는 나의 사전을 잃어버렸다.

I lost _____ dictionary.

**2** 많은 팬들이 그녀를 사랑한다.

Many fans love _____.

**3** 나는 네 도움이 필요해.

I need _____ help.

**4** 그의 개는 흰색이지만 그들의 것은 검은색이다.

His dog is white, but _____ is black.

**5** 너는 그의 전화번호를 알지만, 그는 너의 것을 모른다.

You know his phone number, but he doesn't know _____.

**B** **괄호 안의 대명사를 소유격 또는 소유대명사로 바꾸어 빈칸을 완성하세요.**

**1** It isn't his jacket. It's _____ (I).

**2** They're _____ (we) close friends.

**3** Look at the sky! _____ (it) color is amazing.

**4** This isn't my pencil case. It's _____ (she).

**5** Are they _____ (you) new teachers?

**C**  밑줄 친 부분을 알맞은 형태의 소유격으로 바꿔 쓰세요.

**1** That is her father house. _____

**2** Who's the students homeroom teacher? _____

**3** Do you know John parents? _____

**4** Which of those is the boss car? _____

**5** I read an article about women fashion. _____

**D**  문장의 밑줄 친 부분을 바르게 고쳐 쓰세요.

**1** My sister and me are twins. _____

**2** Lisa didn't invite you and I to her birthday dinner. _____

**3** The teacher stopped his lecture and looked at its. _____

**4** You have a lovely house, and its very clean. _____

**5** The store sells only mens' clothes. _____

## WRITING PRACTICE

우리말과 일치하도록 괄호 안의 말을 이용하여 문장을 완성하세요.

**1** Jason의 두 아이는 동물을 좋아한다. (kids, like animals)

_____.

**2** 그녀는 그를 사랑하지만 그는 그녀를 사랑하지 않는다. (love)

_____, but _____.

**3** 내가 내 열쇠를 어디에 두었더라? (put, key)

_____?

**4** 이 새 공책들은 네 것이니? (new notebooks)

_____?

# UNIT 08 명사의 복수형, 복수형의 발음

☑ **CHECK UP**   **괄호 안에서 알맞은 것을 고르세요.**

**1** Steve has two (car / cars).    `A-1`

**2** Good evening, (ladys / ladies) and gentlemen!    `A-1`

**3** I brush my (tooths / teeth) every day.    `A-2`

**4** Our (childs / children) play a lot of baseball.    `A-2`

**5** There are many (deer / deers) in the forest.    `A-3`

## A   주어진 명사의 복수형을 쓰세요.

**1** apple _____     **2** class _____

**3** dress _____     **4** bench _____

**5** guy _____     **6** family _____

**7** watch _____     **8** holiday _____

**9** city _____     **10** series _____

**11** woman _____     **12** wolf _____

## B   [보기]에서 각각 [z], [s], [iz]로 발음되는 단어를 골라 빈칸에 쓰세요.

[보기]   cup<u>s</u>    potatoe<u>s</u>    wishe<u>s</u>    computer<u>s</u>    park<u>s</u>    matche<u>s</u>

**1** [z]로 발음 → _____

**2** [s]로 발음 → _____

**3** [iz]로 발음 → _____

## C   예시와 같이 그림과 일치하도록 괄호 안의 말을 이용하여 문장을 완성하세요.

**0**

The boy has <u>three tomatoes</u>. (tomato)

**1**

The cook has _____ _____.
(knife)

**2**

The whale ate _____ _____.
(fish)

**3**

_____ _____ are on the farm.
(sheep)

**4**

_____ _____ are on the wall.
(photo)

## WRITING PRACTICE

우리말과 일치하도록 괄호 안의 말을 이용하여 문장을 완성하세요.

**1** 그녀는 하루에 당근을 2개씩 먹는다. (eat, carrot)

She _____ _____ _____ a day.

**2** Brody의 장난감들은 상자 안에 있다. (toy)

_____ _____ _____ in the box.

**3** 원숭이들은 왜 바나나를 좋아할까? (monkey, banana)

_____ _____ _____ love _____?

**4** 우리는 2시간 20분 동안 기다렸다. (hour, minute)

We waited for _____ _____ and _____ _____.

# UNIT 09 There is[are], 명령문, 감탄문

↗ **CHECK UP** 괄호 안에서 알맞은 것을 고르세요.

**1** (Is / Are) there many oranges in the box?  `A`

**2** (Be / Do) honest.  `B-1`

**3** (Don't / Not) be rude to others.  `B-2`

**4** (Not let's / Let's not) talk about it.  `B-3`

**5** (What / How) a good actor he is!  `C`

**A** 그림과 일치하도록 「There is / are / isn't / aren't」를 이용하여 문장을 완성하세요.

**1** _____ a bed in the room.

**2** _____ any chairs in the room.

**3** _____ some books on the bed.

**4** _____ an air conditioner in the room.

**5** _____ a cat under the table.

**6** _____ any people in the room.

**B** [보기]에서 알맞은 것을 하나씩 골라 빈칸을 채우세요.

[보기]   Don't use   Open   Be   Let's   Don't take

**1** _____ quiet, please.

**2** _____ cell phones in the theater.

**3** _____ photos in the museum.

**4** _____ your mouth wide.

**5** _____ do it together, right now.

**C** 각 명령문 다음에 올 가장 알맞은 말을 하나씩 짝지으세요.

1 Hurry up! •          • (a) A car is coming.
2 Watch out! •          • (b) There's plenty of food.
3 Enjoy! •          • (c) I need you.
4 Don't be afraid. •          • (d) We'll help you.
5 Please don't leave me. •          • (e) We're late.

**D** 예시와 같이 우리말과 일치하도록 괄호 안의 말을 강조하는 감탄문을 완성하세요.

0 매우 완벽한 날씨구나! (weather)
   <u>What perfect weather it is</u>!

1 저 말은 정말 빠르게 달리는구나! (fast)
   _____ _____ that horse _____!

2 정말 특별한 선물들이구나! (gifts)
   _____ special _____ they _____!

3 그녀는 정말 어리석었구나! (foolish)
   _____ _____ she _____!

## WRITING PRACTICE

우리말과 일치하도록 괄호 안의 말을 바르게 배열하여 문장을 완성하세요.

1 음식을 버리지 마라. (throw away, food, don't)
   → _____.

2 오늘 밤에는 나가지 말자. (tonight, not, go out, let's)
   → _____.

3 이 도시에는 대학이 몇 개 있나요? (universities, are, how many, there)
   → _____ in this city?

4 그들은 얼마나 시끄러운 남자애들이던지! (noisy, what, boys, were, they)
   → _____!

# UNIT 10 동사와 문장 성분

정답 및 해설 p.14

## ☑ CHECK UP 괄호 안에서 알맞은 것을 고르세요.

**1** Adam gave lilies (to / for) her.  `B`

**2** My father made this chair (to / for) me.  `B`

**3** You look (sad / sadly).  `C-1`

**4** Mark wants his son (clear / to clear) the table.  `C-2`

**5** Please let me (know / to know) your address.  `C-2`

## A 예시와 같이 두 목적어의 위치를 바꾸어 문장을 다시 쓰세요.

**0** Send Mary the message.

  → Send the message to Mary.

**1** I'll make some cookies for you.

  → _____

**2** Could you buy a cup of coffee for me?

  → _____

**3** Would you give me another chance?

  → _____

**4** Carol lent Bob money.

  → _____

## B 괄호 안에서 알맞은 것을 고르세요.

**1** The soup smells (good / well).

**2** She keeps her hands (clean / cleanly).

**3** It's 12:30 p.m., and I'm getting (hungry / hungrily).

**4** I felt (bad / badly) when I woke up today.

**5** It may sound (strange / strangely), but it's true!

**6** He found the princess (beautiful / beautifully).

**C**   문장의 밑줄 친 부분을 바르게 고쳐 쓰세요.

**1**  My doctor advised me start exercising.  _____

**2**  The teacher made them to do their homework.  _____

**3**  Who told you done this?  _____

**4**  I expected her helped me.  _____

**5**  Mom didn't let me to go out after dark.  _____


**D**   [보기]에서 알맞은 것을 하나씩 골라 빈칸을 채우세요.

[보기]   reached   raised   lied   lay   laid   rose

**1**  Eva _____ her head when I called her.

**2**  The paper _____ on his desk.

**3**  Joseph _____ his coat on the sofa.

**4**  The temperature _____ to 40 °C last summer.

**5**  I don't trust him because he _____ to me.

**6**  We _____ San Diego just before midnight.


## WRITING PRACTICE

우리말과 일치하도록 괄호 안의 말을 바르게 배열하여 문장을 완성하세요.

**1**  Helen은 아이들에게 영어를 가르친다. (English, teaches, children)

→ Helen _____.

**2**  그녀는 나를 웃게 만들기 때문에 나는 그녀를 좋아한다. (laugh, she, me, makes)

→ I like her because _____.

**3**  내게 그 사건의 진실을 말해 줘. (the truth, me, tell, please)

→ _____ about the accident.

**4**  나는 그녀가 Henry와 함께 거기에 서 있는 것을 보았다. (saw, standing, I, there, her)

→ _____ with Henry.

**1** 다음 짝지어진 동사의 현재형-과거형의 형태가 옳지 <u>않은</u> 것을 고르세요.

① eat – ate
② play – plaied
③ carry – carried
④ stop – stopped
⑤ cut – cut

**2** 다음 짝지어진 명사의 단수형-복수형의 형태가 옳지 <u>않은</u> 것을 고르세요.

① dish – dishes
② thief – thieves
③ mouse – mice
④ leaf – leafs
⑤ toy – toys

서술형

**3** 다음 빈칸에 알맞은 be동사를 쓰세요.

James and I _____ good friends.
We always go jogging together.

**4** 다음 빈칸에 들어갈 수 <u>없는</u> 말을 고르세요.

Later, she became _____.

① a teacher
② healthy
③ happily
④ smart
⑤ a famous doctor

**[5-6]** 다음 밑줄 친 부분 중 어법상 옳지 <u>않은</u> 것을 고르세요.

**5** ① The baby <u>cries</u> a lot.
② Peter <u>watches</u> TV every day.
③ Nilson <u>haves</u> many books at home.
④ Janet sometimes <u>washes</u> the dishes.
⑤ Jongmi <u>goes</u> to Seoul Middle School.

**6** ① We <u>talked</u> a lot about our life.
② Amy <u>was</u> one of my classmates.
③ She <u>readed</u> a lot of books in the library.
④ I <u>graduated</u> from ABC university.
⑤ I <u>liked</u> her because she did her best on everything.

**7** 다음 중 자연스럽지 <u>않은</u> 대화를 고르세요.

① A: Are you from China?
   B: Yes, I'm Chinese.
② A: Don't you have a pet?
   B: No, I have a dog.
③ A: Is everything all right?
   B: Yes, it is.
④ A: Wasn't the movie fun?
   B: Yes, it was really fun.
⑤ A: Did Liz go to the concert?
   B: No, she was busy.

**[8-10] 다음 중 어법상 옳은 것을 고르세요.**

**8** ① Its my pencil case.
② His tall and smart.
③ I'am a soccer player.
④ We'ar good at math.
⑤ They're students from Mexico.

**9** ① Is she do her homework?
② Were I good in the play?
③ Don't she have free time?
④ Was Patrick and I in the list?
⑤ Did she use my computer?

**10** ① I put.
② Rise your hand.
③ The food tastes nicely.
④ The boy looked strong.
⑤ They let me to sing.

**11** 다음 표지판을 발견할 가능성이 가장 높은 장소를 고르세요.

- Do not litter.
- Don't talk loudly.
- Show your ticket at the front door.
- Turn off your phone during the performance.

① In a train          ② In school
③ On a bus           ④ In a theater
⑤ In a swimming pool

**[12-13] 다음 중 우리말을 영어로 바르게 옮긴 것을 고르세요.**

**12** ① Charlie의 초콜렛은 아주 맛있다.
→ Charlie chocolate is so delicious.
② 그의 셔츠는 붉은 색이고, 내 것은 파란색이다.
→ His shirt is red, and mine is blue.
③ 수미는 그에게 꽃을 주었다.
→ Sumi gave his flowers.
④ 내 고양이의 이름은 나비이고, 그것의 털은 흰색이다.
→ My cat's name is Nabi, and it's fur is white.
⑤ Monica는 책을 한 권 썼다. 그녀의 책은 재미있다.
→ Monica wrote a book. Hers book is interesting.

**13** ① 너는 나에게 3시에 전화했니?
→ Do you call me at three?
② 여기가 어디인가요?
→ Where goes here?
③ Kate는 왜 아이스크림을 싫어하니?
→ Why Kate hates ice cream?
④ 저 사람 John 아니니?
→ Isn't that John?
⑤ 이것은 누구의 가방이니?
→ Is this bag whose?

서술형
**14** 다음 괄호 안의 말을 알맞은 형태로 바꾸어 빈칸을 완성하세요.

In England, there (1) _____ (be) sometimes four (2) _____ (season) in one day.

**15** ① Sumin doesn't like pizza.
   ② Jack is not a violin player.
   ③ We didn't have a good time.
   ④ Sarah doesn't tell lies to me.
   ⑤ Jason and I didn't sang together.

**16** ① School isn't over.
   ② Chickens don't fly.
   ③ She doesn't cleans windows.
   ④ Sam and Tom didn't like the cookies.
   ⑤ There weren't many flowers in the garden.

**17** ① Show me your maps.
   ② Where are the babies?
   ③ I have two pianos at home.
   ④ I have two more classes today.
   ⑤ There are three beautiful womans in red.

**18** ① Don't noisy. Be quiet.
   ② Move faster! Be quick!
   ③ Welcome! Please come in.
   ④ Do not open the red door.
   ⑤ Never tell my secret to anyone.

**19** 다음 밑줄 친 부분이 가리키는 것이 나머지와 다른 하나를 고르세요.

> Last summer I bought a new watch. ① <u>It</u> was silver and shiny. I liked ② <u>it</u> because ③ <u>it</u> looked beautiful. But something sad happened. My baby sister broke ④ <u>it</u>. ⑤ <u>It's</u> also my fault because I didn't keep an eye on it.

①     ②     ③     ④     ⑤

**20** 다음 중 자연스러운 대화를 모두 고르세요. (2개)

   ① A: Where is he having lunch?
      B: Because he feels hungry.
   ② A: When do you go to school?
      B: By bicycle.
   ③ A: Whose is the ruler?
      B: This is Tina, my friend.
   ④ A: How often do you watch movies?
      B: Once a month.
   ⑤ A: Which do you like better, dogs or cats?
      B: I like both, equally.

서술형

**21** 다음 빈칸에 공통으로 들어갈 말을 쓰세요.

> • _____ are students in the playground.
> • Is _____ a post office around here?

**22** 다음 중 괄호 안의 동사를 빈칸에 현재분사 형태로 쓸 수 있는 것을 고르세요.

   ① I saw you _____ (dance) last night.
   ② Mr. James told us _____ (write) it down.
   ③ Please let me _____ (introduce) my sister.
   ④ She asked me _____ (buy) tickets for her.
   ⑤ You can't make me _____ (do) that.

Jonathan is a *seagull. But he is different from other seagulls. He ① likes to fly. He wants to fly higher.

"② There is a big mountain near the seashore. I will fly over it," he said.

His only friend ③ said, "But it sounds ④ dangerously." He ⑤ answered, "Yes, but I want to try new things. I _____ (not/ want) to live like others."

*seagull 갈매기

**23** 위 글의 밑줄 친 부분 중 어법상 옳지 <u>않은</u> 것을 고르세요.

①      ②      ③      ④      ⑤

서술형

**24** 괄호 안의 not/want를 알맞은 형태로 바꿔 쓰세요.

서술형

**25** 다음 우리말과 일치하도록 괄호 안의 말을 이용하여 문장을 완성하세요.

와, 얼마나 멋진 경기였던지! (interesting, was)

→ Wow, _____ _____ _____ game it _____!

[26-27] 다음 글을 읽고, 물음에 답하세요.

What do I want to be? Let me tell you about my father first. My father is a teacher. He loves _____ (child), and he likes to teach them. I respect my father very much. So I want to become a teacher like him.

서술형

**26** 괄호 안의 child를 알맞은 형태로 바꿔 쓰세요.

**27** 다음 중 위 글의 화자에 대한 설명으로 옳지 <u>않은</u> 것을 고르세요.

① 화자는 자신의 아버지를 존경한다.
② 화자의 아버지는 교사이다.
③ 화자의 아버지는 아이들을 사랑한다.
④ 화자는 아이들을 가르치는 것을 좋아한다.
⑤ 화자는 자신의 꿈에 대해 이야기 하고 있다.

**28** 다음 중 어법상 옳지 <u>않은</u> 문장을 고르세요.

① Tommy always buys fruit at this supermarket. ② I also like fruit very much. ③ So we often come here together. ④ Jenny sometimes join us. ⑤ Tommy, Jenny, and I eat lots of fruit every day.

①      ②      ③      ④      ⑤

# UNIT 11 시제의 개념, 현재시제, 과거시제

**☑ CHECK UP** 괄호 안에서 알맞은 것을 고르세요.

**1** I always (do / does) my homework after school. <kbd>B</kbd>

**2** Banks (don't / doesn't) open on weekends. <kbd>B</kbd>

**3** The Spanish artist Picasso (is / was) born in 1881. <kbd>C</kbd>

**4** Ryan (works / worked) very late last night. <kbd>C</kbd>

## A

[보기]에서 알맞은 동사를 골라 현재시제로 바꾸어 빈칸을 채우세요.

[보기]  play    grow    ask    speak    go

**1** My friends and I _____ soccer every Saturday.

**2** Fei never _____ Chinese at work.

**3** Her little brother always _____ her many questions.

**4** Sarah _____ to Oxford to see her mother twice a week.

**5** The plant _____ well in the yard.

## B

괄호 안의 동사를 현재시제 또는 과거시제로 바꾸어 문장을 완성하세요.

**1** Last year I _____ (go) to Jeju Island with my friends.

**2** My father usually _____ (wake) up at seven.

**3** Now Paul _____ (work) as a web designer for the company.

**4** I _____ (talk) with my parents about my dream last night.

**5** She _____ (bite) her nails when she gets angry.

**6** He _____ (found) the hospital in 1980.

**7** I _____ (meet) my old friend Annie a week ago.

**C** 괄호 안에서 알맞은 것을 고르세요.

**1** I (waited / wait / will wait) two hours for you yesterday.

**2** He (arrived / arrives / is arriving) home two hours ago.

**3** Harry (come / comes / will come) from England and now lives in Korea.

**4** It got very cold, and the water in the Han River (freeze / froze / frozen).

**5** Amy (exercised / exercises / will exercise) for one hour every morning these days.

**D** 어법상 틀린 부분을 고쳐 문장을 다시 쓰세요.

**1** Beijing was in China.

→ _____

**2** The bus come every five minutes.

→ _____

**3** He goes to church last Sunday.

→ _____

**4** Nowadays Michael kept a diary.

→ _____

## WRITING PRACTICE

우리말과 일치하도록 괄호 안의 말을 이용하여 문장을 완성하세요.

**1** 물은 섭씨 100도에서 끓는다. (boil)

_____ _____ at 100 ˚C.

**2** Jackson은 매일 8시에 일어난다. (get up)

_____ _____ _____ at 8 o'clock every day.

**3** 그녀는 그저께 악몽을 꾸었다. (have a nightmare)

_____ _____ _____ _____ the day before yesterday.

**4** 나는 작년에 쿠바에 갔다. (go)

_____ _____ to Cuba _____ _____.

# UNIT 12 미래시제

정답 및 해설 p.19

**괄호 안에서 알맞은 것을 고르세요.**

**1** He'll (wins / win) the game.    `A - 1`

**2** A: Would you like an apple juice or an orange juice?    `A - 2`

    B : (I'll / I'm going to) have an apple juice.

**3** I am going (visit / to visit) my grandmother this weekend.    `A - 3`

**4** The semester (ends / has ended) on July 16.    `B`

**5** If she (goes / will go) there, she'll meet him.    `C`

## A

**주어진 말을 바르게 배열하여 문장을 완성하세요.**

**1** the bus / will / I / take

→ _____ .

**2** I / not / to her / will / again / speak

→ _____ .

**3** begin / the class / going / is / to

→ _____ soon.

**4** He / going / call / is / to / not / me

→ _____ .

## B

**be going to와 괄호 안의 말을 이용하여 문장을 완성하세요.**

**1** They _____ (go) to Taiwan tomorrow.

**2** He _____ (cook) Indian curry tonight.

**3** We _____ (buy) a car next month.

**4** I _____ (not, study) on my summer vacation.

**5** Tom _____ (not, bother) Jerry anymore.

**C** 괄호 안에서 알맞은 것을 고르세요.

**1** If we (hurry / will hurry / hurrying) now, we'll get there on time.

**2** If Bob (will try / tries / try) hard, he'll save money.

**3** When you (came / come / will come) back, I'll give you a big hug.

**4** As soon as I (will arrive / arrive / arrived), I'll visit you.

**D** 괄호 안의 동사를 알맞은 형태로 바꾸어 대화를 완성하세요.

Waiter : Would you like some dessert or coffee?

Alice : Yes. I ⓐ _____ (have) coffee, please.

Mia : I ⓑ _____ (have) the same.

Alice : So, what are you going to do this weekend?

Mia : I ⓒ _____ (watch) a movie with Becky. Do you want to join us? She wants to see you again!

Alice : Wow, with Becky? If she ⓓ _____ (come), I ⓔ _____ (go) with you.

---

우리말과 일치하도록 괄호 안의 말을 이용하여 문장을 완성하세요.

**1** Jenny가 이번 주 일요일에 결혼한다. (get married)

Jenny is _____ _____ this Sunday.

**2** 네가 안 가면 나도 안 갈 거야. (go, will)

If you _____ _____, I _____, either.

**3** 첫 기차는 오전 5시 30분에 떠난다. (leave)

_____ _____ _____ _____ at 5:30 a.m.

**4** 너는 언제 네 여자친구에게 전화할 거니? (going, call)

When _____ _____ _____ _____ _____ your girlfriend?

↗ **CHECK UP**

**괄호 안에서 알맞은 것을 고르세요.**

**1** Look! He (comes / is coming) out of the house.　A

**2** We (watch / were watching) TV when the doorbell rang.　B

**3** I (understand / am understanding) how you feel.　C

**4** This music (sounds / is sounding) so good.　C

**A**

**그림과 일치하도록 [보기]에서 동사를 하나씩 골라 진행형으로 바꾸어 문장을 완성하세요.**

[보기]　have　brush　sit　do

**1**

He _____ his teeth now.

**2**

Jinny _____ dinner with her family now.

**3**

I _____ my homework when my sister came to my room with a book.

**4**

Tomorrow afternoon at 14:00, we _____ in an airplane to Paris.

**B** 문장이 미래를 나타내면 F를, 현재진행형이면 P를 쓰세요.

**1** I'm going home in two days.          _____

**2** What is he doing now?          _____

**3** The baby is not sleeping right now.          _____

**4** I'm going fishing with my father this weekend.          _____


**C** 어법상 <u>틀린</u> 부분을 고쳐 문장을 다시 쓰세요.

**1** This watermelon is tasting good.

→ _____

**2** My mother is knowing a lot about food.

→ _____

**3** She will be not using the car.

→ _____

**4** It is meaning nothing to me.

→ _____


## WRITING PRACTICE

괄호 안의 말을 써서 다음 [조건]에 맞는 문장을 완성하세요.

[조건]  현재진행형, 과거진행형, 미래진행형을 각각 한 번씩 사용할 것

**1** 내일 이 시간이면 나는 집에서 영화를 보고 있을 것이다. (watch)

This time tomorrow I _____ _____ _____ a movie at home.

**2** 그가 누군가와 전화 통화를 하고 있다. (talk on the phone)

He _____ _____ _____ _____ _____ with someone.

**3** 그 사건이 벌어졌을 때 당신은 무엇을 하고 있었습니까? (do, happen)

_____ _____ _____ _____ when the accident _____?

# UNIT 14 현재완료형

정답 및 해설 p.21

CHECK UP  괄호 안에서 알맞은 것을 고르세요.

**1** He (went / has gone) to India in 2012.  `A-2`

**2** When (did you start / have you started) your blog?  `A-2`

**3** My sister has lived in Rome (for / since) 2010.  `B-1`

**4** She (has / have) never seen an elephant.  `B-3`

**5** I (have / did) already booked my ticket to Madrid.  `B-4`

## A  괄호 안의 동사를 현재완료형으로 바꾸어 문장을 완성하세요.

**1** I _____ (speak) to the boss about my summer vacation.

**2** They _____ (not eat) anything since Monday.

**3** Angela _____ (forget) the face of her mother.

**4** I _____ (be) to New York three times, and I loved it!

## B  질문과 대답을 바르게 짝짓고, 아래에서 대화와 일치하는 내용을 고르세요.

**1** Can I speak with Dr. Lee? •     • (a) She has just left the office.

**2** Where is your pencil? •     • (b) No, I have never even seen him.

**3** Have you ever met the •     • (c) Someone has taken it.
       president before?

**1** ⓐ Dr. Lee is at the office.   ⓑ Dr. Lee isn't at the office.   ⓒ Dr. Lee will be back soon.

**2** ⓐ I have the pencil.   ⓑ I will buy a new pencil.   ⓒ I don't have the pencil.

**3** ⓐ I haven't met him.   ⓑ I met the president.   ⓒ I'm going to meet him.

**C**    괄호 안에서 알맞은 것을 고르세요.

**1** Lucy has (catches / caught / catched) a cold.

**2** Darcy has taught English (for / since / during) two years.

**3** George has (yet / ever / just) arrived home.

**4** He (didn't speak / hasn't spoken / isn't speaking) to her since March.

**5** I've missed Jimmy (for / since / by) he left Korea.

**D**    어법상 **틀린** 부분을 고쳐 문장을 다시 쓰세요.

**1** What have you done last night?

→ _____

**2** My father has needed this newspaper this morning.

→ _____

**3** Mr. and Mrs. Smith have come here yesterday.

→ _____

**4** I have finished my homework an hour ago.

→ _____

## WRITING PRACTICE

우리말과 일치하도록 괄호 안의 말을 바르게 배열하여 문장을 완성하세요.

**1** 나는 남아프리카에 갔다 왔다. (to, have, South Africa, been)

I _____ .

**2** 요가 수업을 들어본 적 있으세요? (taken, you, ever, have, a yoga class)

_____ ?

**3** 에이미는 지금 여기에 없다. 그녀는 슈퍼마켓에 갔다. (the supermarket, she, has, to, gone)

Amy is not here now. _____ .

**4** 이 책이 출판된 지 1년이 되었다. (a year, since, has, this book, was published, been)

It _____ .

☑ **CHECK UP**  괄호 안에서 알맞은 것을 고르세요.

**1** I (have had / have been having) this camera for 10 years.  `A`

**2** Rebecca (will have waited / has been waiting) for the bus for 20 minutes.  `A`

**3** When I got home, a parcel (has / had) arrived.  `B`

**4** When Edward arrived at the store, the coat (has / had) already been sold out.  `B`

**5** He will (have / has) arrived at the train station by now.  `C`

**A**  예시와 같이 **for** 또는 **since**와 괄호 안의 말을 이용하여 질문에 답하세요.

**0**  Q : How long have you been going to this school? (September)
A : I have been going to this school since September.

**1**  Q : How long have you been teaching history? (eight years)
A : _____

**2**  Q : How long have you been living in this town? (last year)
A : _____

**3**  Q : How long have you been playing the violin? (ten years)
A : _____

**4**  Q : How long have you been talking on the phone? (an hour)
A : _____

**5**  Q : How long have you been watching TV? (3 o'clock)
A : _____

**B**  [보기]에서 알맞은 말을 골라 과거완료형으로 바꾸어 문장을 완성하세요.

[보기]  not/take     lose     hike

**1**  Jay was tired because he _____ all day.

**2**  Jenny got wet in the rain because she _____ her umbrella.

**3**  Liz didn't tell anybody how she _____ her money.

**C** 괄호 안의 동사를 미래형(will + 동사원형) 또는 미래완료형으로 바꾸어 문장을 완성하세요.

**1** My car isn't working, so we _____ (take) the train.

**2** Call me after 2 p.m. We _____ (finish) lunch by then.

**3** Next month Jake _____ (work) with us for ten years.

**4** Next year my parents _____ (be married) for 15 years.

**D** 괄호 안에서 알맞은 것을 고르세요.

**1** I (looked / have been looking / will have looked) for a job since August.

**2** Kevin (played / has been playing / was playing) golf since he was twelve.

**3** By the end of the day, the doctor (sees / is seeing / will have seen) twenty patients.

**4** He didn't receive the letter that I (send / had sent / will have sent) to him.

**5** Before Jina went to France last week, she (will never be / never had been / had never been) outside Korea.

---

**WRITING PRACTICE**

우리말과 일치하도록 괄호 안의 말을 이용하여 문장을 완성하세요.

**1** 그녀는 부산에서 일한 지 얼마나 되었나요? (how long, work)

_____ _____ _____ _____ _____ _____ in Busan?

**2** 내가 버스정류장에 도착했을 때, 버스는 벌써 떠나버렸다. (leave, get to)

The bus _____ already _____ when I _____ _____ the bus stop.

**3** 내가 그 영화를 한 번 더 보면, 그것을 네 번 본 것이 된다. (see)

If I _____ the film once more, I _____ _____ _____ it four times.

**4** 내가 TV를 켰을 때 그 프로그램은 이미 끝나 있었다. (turn on, end)

When I _____ _____ the TV, the program _____ already _____.

☑ **CHECK UP**   괄호 안에서 알맞은 것을 고르세요.

**1** Leo couldn't (find / finds) his wallet anywhere.   `A - 2`

**2** Douglas (can't / couldn't) visit us the day before yesterday.   `B - 1`

**3** Next week you'll (can / be able to) get a ticket to the concert.   `B - 2`

**4** Jody isn't answering the phone. She (must / can't) be sleeping.   `C - 1`

**5** Joe (must / can't) be in Indonesia. I've just seen him in Seoul.   `C - 3`

**A**   [보기]에서 알맞은 말을 하나씩 골라 빈칸을 채우세요.

> [보기]   can   can't   could   couldn't   be able to

**1** Elsa, _____ you speak Korean?

**2** Next year I will _____ drive.

**3** When my brother was a baby, I _____ hold him with one arm.

**4** His legs are broken. He _____ walk now.

**5** Martin and Anika were really busy, so they _____ come to my birthday party.

**B**   빈칸에 must 또는 can't를 알맞게 쓰세요.

**1** Your bag is full of books! It _____ be very heavy.

**2** Dinner _____ be ready. Mom is setting the table.

**3** He _____ be tired. He has done a lot of work.

**4** Esther _____ be over thirty. She looks so young.

**5** It _____ be his birthday. People are giving him gifts.

**6** We _____ be late. We left the house on time.

**C** 두 문장이 같은 뜻이 되도록 may, must, can't를 이용하여 문장을 완성하세요.

**1** Perhaps this story is true.

= This story _____ _____ true.

**2** He is certainly not an Englishman.

= He _____ _____ an Englishman.

**3** That is surely Ben's girlfriend.

= That _____ _____ Ben's girlfriend.

**4** I'm sure that he loves her.

= He _____ _____ her.


**D** 괄호 안에서 알맞은 것을 고르세요.

**1** This jacket (can't / may / must) be Paul's. It's too big to him.

**2** I'm not sure, but Mike (can't / may / must) be at the gym.

**3** The pianist won't (can / able to / be able to) perform tonight. She is very sick now.

**4** He (could / couldn't / was able to) finish his paper because he didn't have enough time.

**5** Plants (can't / must not / be able to) live without water.


## WRITING PRACTICE

우리말과 일치하도록 [보기]와 괄호 안의 말을 이용하여 문장을 완성하세요.

[보기]   must      can't      may

**1** 너 설마 진심은 아니겠지! 정말 그런 의미는 아니지, 그렇지? (serious)

You _____ _____ _____! You don't really mean it, do you?

**2** 그 질문은 쉽게 들리지만, 아이들에게는 그것이 어려울지도 모른다. (difficult)

The question sounds easy, but for children, it _____ _____ _____.

**3** 그는 엑스트라 라지 사이즈 피자 한 판을 주문했다. 그는 배고픈 게 틀림없다. (hungry)

He ordered an extra-large pizza. _____ _____ _____ _____.

정답 및 해설 p.25

↗ **CHECK UP** 괄호 안에서 알맞은 것을 고르세요.

**1** (Could / Would) I have more information about the class?  `A-1`

**2** (May I / May you) come in?  `A-2`

**3** (Will I / Will you) shut the door, please?  `B-1`

**4** (Would / Could) you like to dance with me?  `B-1`

**5** (Shall / Would) we have chicken or pasta for dinner?  `B-3`

**A** 예시와 같이 Can 또는 Could를 사용하여 각 명령문을 ⓘ 또는 ⓕ 형태로 바꿔 쓰세요. (ⓘ는 친한 사이에서, ⓕ는 조금 더 공손하게 요청할 경우에 씀)

**0** Open the window. → ⓘ Can you open the window?

  Help me. → ⓕ Could you help me?

**1** Tell me your address. → ⓕ _____ ?

**2** Wait for me. → ⓘ _____ ?

**3** Fill out this form. → ⓕ _____ ?

**4** Change this money into dollars. → ⓘ _____ ?

**B** [보기]에서 알맞은 동사를 하나씩 골라 빈칸을 채우세요.

[보기]  drive    help    give    lend    send    tell

**1** Would you _____ me an email right now?

**2** Can you _____ me where the city library is?

**3** Would you _____ me to the airport tomorrow morning?

**4** Could you _____ me your bike for a couple of days?

**5** Would you _____ me a hint to solve the problem?

**6** Will you _____ me move these boxes?

**C**   예시와 같이 주어진 말과 「shall we ~?」를 써서 문장을 완성하세요.

**0** when / meet again?  →  When shall we meet again?

**1** what / eat for lunch  →  _____?

**2** how / travel to Dok-do  →  _____?

**3** what / do on the weekend  →  _____?

**4** where / go this summer  →  _____?

**5** what time / leave tomorrow  →  _____?


**D**   괄호 안에서 어법상 적절하지 <u>않은</u> 하나를 고르세요.

**1** (Can I / May I / Would I) ask your age?

**2** (Do you like / How about / Would you like) going shopping?

**3** A : Could I speak with you for a moment?
   B : (Yes, you can / Yes, you could / No problem).


## WRITING PRACTICE

우리말과 일치하도록 [보기]와 괄호 안의 말을 이용하여 문장을 완성하세요.

[보기]  like   use   walk   turn off

**1** 화장실 좀 써도 될까요? (may)
_____ _____ _____ the bathroom?

**2** 에어컨을 꺼 주시겠어요? (could)
_____ _____ _____ the air conditioner, please?

**3** 저와 함께 영화 보러 가실래요? (would)
_____ _____ to go to the movies with me?

**4** 우리 공원에서 걸을까? (shall)
_____ _____ _____ in the park?

정답 및 해설 p.27

☑ **CHECK UP**   괄호 안에서 알맞은 것을 고르세요.

**1** We'll (must / have to) clean the floor before Mom comes.    `A-2`

**2** You (must not / don't have to) help me. I can do it alone.    `A-3`

**3** The tea is too hot. You (must not / don't have to) drink it yet.    `A-3`

**4** You (ought not to / not ought to) drink so much coke.    `B-2`

**5** You (had better not / don't have better) wear shoes in the house.    `B-3`

**A**   [보기]에서 알맞은 말을 골라 빈칸을 채우세요.

[보기]   have to      has to      had to

**1** I _____ call my mom right now. If I don't, she will be worried.

**2** She _____ get a visa before she goes abroad.

**3** Ann _____ walk to work yesterday because her car didn't start.

**4** The weather is really bad today. We may _____ cancel our flight.

**5** We _____ change our plan when it rained.

**B**   [보기]에서 알맞은 말을 골라 빈칸을 채우세요.

[보기]   must      must not      don't have to

**1** You _____ be late on the first day of your new job.

**2** I _____ mail this letter today. It's urgent.

**3** We _____ work tomorrow. It's a national holiday.

**4** You _____ worry about it. I'll take care of it.

**5** We _____ be careful when we cross the street.

**6** You _____ throw trash on the street.

**C**  should 또는 shouldn't와 [보기]의 동사를 하나씩 써서 문장을 완성하세요.

[보기]  drink    drive    eat    give

**1** You _____ your password to anyone.

**2** You _____ plenty of water every day. It's good for your health.

**3** You _____ carefully in school zones.

**4** You _____ too much meat. It'll make you fat.


**D**  괄호 안에서 알맞은 것을 고르세요.

**1** Sue (has to / must / had to) study for a test last night.

**2** You (must / had to / don't need to) walk to school. You can take the bus.

**3** People (should / must not / don't need to) use cell phones while they are driving.

**4** You (had not better / had better not / hadn't better) tell me any lies.

**5** (Do / Does / Is) she have to take vitamin E?


## WRITING PRACTICE

우리말과 일치하도록 괄호 안의 말을 바르게 배열하여 문장을 완성하세요.

**1** 극장 안에 들어가려면 표가 있어야 한다. (the theater, must, a ticket, you, have, to get in)

→ _____.

**2** 우산을 가져가는 게 좋을 거야. 밖에 비가 많이 와. (better, had, take, your umbrella, you)

→ _____. It is raining a lot outside.

**3** 밤에는 커피를 마시지 않는 것이 좋다. (drink, not, coffee, should, you)

→ _____ at night.

**4** 그것을 좋아하지 않으면 안 먹어도 된다. (have, don't, eat, you, it, to)

→ _____ if you don't like it.

# UNIT 19 습관·상태의 조동사, 조동사 + have v-ed

정답 및 해설 p.28

↗ **CHECK UP** 괄호 안에서 알맞은 것을 고르세요.

**1** She (used to / would) be a florist, but she's a barista in a coffee shop now. `A-2`

**2** You may (drop / have dropped) your purse somewhere yesterday. `B-1`

**3** I didn't hear the doorbell. I must (be / have been) asleep. `B-2`

**4** You can't (see / have seen) me. I was not there at that time. `B-3`

**5** I should not (eat / have eaten) so much chocolate last night. `B-4`

**A** 밑줄 친 조동사의 의미로 옳은 것을 [보기]에서 하나씩 골라 쓰세요.

[보기]  확실한 추측     부정적인 추측     불확실한 추측     아쉬움

**1** Julia <u>may</u> have done what I said. _____

**2** Julia <u>must</u> have done what I said. _____

**3** Julia <u>can't</u> have done what I said. _____

**4** Julia <u>should</u> have done what I said. _____

**B** 우리말과 일치하도록 문장의 밑줄 친 부분을 바르게 고쳐 쓰세요.

**1** 너는 모자를 썼어야 했다. 너는 심하게 탔다.

You <u>should wear</u> a hat. You were badly burnt. _____

**2** 길이 젖었다. 비가 왔었음이 틀림없다.

The road is wet. It <u>must rain</u>. _____

**3** 너는 그 파티를 일찍 떠나지 말았어야 했다.

You <u>should have not left</u> the party early. _____

**4** Jack은 회의를 잊어버렸을지도 모른다. 그는 어제 그곳에 참석하지 않았다.

Jack <u>may forget</u> about the meeting. He didn't attend it yesterday.

_____

**48** G-ZONE WORKBOOK

**C** [보기]에서 알맞은 말을 하나씩 골라 빈칸을 채우세요.

[보기]   may not   must   can't   should   would

**1** Cecil failed the exam. He _____ have studied harder.

**2** Tony is a very nice man. He _____ have done such a bad thing.

**3** I remember his face. I _____ have seen him before.

**4** His story was interesting, but it _____ have been true.

**5** My grandfather _____ tell me funny stories when I was young.

**D** 괄호 안에서 알맞은 것을 고르세요.

**1** I used to (be / being) a Boy Scout in elementary school.

**2** She (may have not / may not have) taken her car key.

**3** The building (would / used to) be a train station, but it is empty now.

**4** I stayed up too late last night. I (should / shouldn't) have drunk coffee at 11 p.m.

**5** I heard they lost all of their luggage. Their trip (must / can't) have been terrible.

## WRITING PRACTICE

우리말과 일치하도록 괄호 안의 말을 이용하여 문장을 완성하세요.

**1** 나는 좀 더 조심했어야 했다. (be more careful)

I _____ _____ _____ _____ _____.

**2** Lisa는 옷에 많은 돈을 쓰곤 했지만, 지금은 그렇지 않다. (spend)

Lisa _____ _____ _____ a lot of money on clothes, but now she doesn't.

**3** Audrey는 알람 시계 소리를 듣지 못했는지도 모른다. (hear)

Audrey _____ _____ _____ _____ the alarm clock.

**4** Max는 시속 150km로 차를 몰지 말았어야 했다. (drive)

Max _____ _____ _____ 150 km an hour.

# UNIT 20 수동태의 개념 및 형태

정답 및 해설 p.29

**☑ CHECK UP** 괄호 안에서 알맞은 것을 고르세요.

**1** Chocolate milk (invented / was invented) in Jamaica. `A-2`

**2** This tree (planted / was planted) by my grandfather. `A-2`

**3** I (wasn't invited / didn't invite) to the party. `B-1`

**4** This ticket can (exchange / be exchanged) for a special gift. `B-2`

**5** He (laughed at / was laughed at) by everyone at the meeting. `B-3`

## A
각 문장을 수동태 문장으로 바꿔 쓰세요.

**1** The children are drawing pictures in pencil.

→ Pictures _____.

**2** The dog dug a hole in the yard.

→ A hole _____.

**3** My team will win first prize.

→ First prize _____.

**4** Smith has cut down the apple tree.

→ The apple tree _____.

## B
괄호 안의 말을 바르게 배열하여 문장을 완성하세요.

**1** (by, invented, Alexander Graham Bell, was)

→ The telephone _____.

**2** (bought, were, Italy, in)

→ Her clothes _____.

**3** (Germany, made, in, was)

→ The movie _____.

**4** (is, hired, going to, by the company, be)

→ Helen _____.

## C 문장의 밑줄 친 부분을 바르게 고쳐 쓰세요.

**1** Real love <u>can't buy</u> by money.  _____

**2** The house has already <u>been sell</u>.  _____

**3** My grandmother will <u>look after</u> by me.  _____

**4** What <u>can done</u> by the man?  _____

**5** The event <u>may hold</u> in the park.  _____

## D 괄호 안에서 알맞은 것을 고르세요.

**1** My cat (was run / was run over / was ran over) by a car.

**2** I (am / was / will be) introduced to him by George at a party last year.

**3** He will (have picked up / be picked up / be pick up) tomorrow at the airport.

**4** The road (is repaired / is being repaired / is been repairing), so no cars can use it now.

**5** The police reported that some jewelry had (be stolen / been stole / been stolen).

**6** The shocking news is going to (announced / be announced / been announced) soon.

---

## WRITING PRACTICE

우리말과 일치하도록 괄호 안의 말을 바르게 배열하여 문장을 완성하세요.

**1** 에펠탑은 구스타브 에펠에 의해 설계되었다. (was, the Eiffel Tower, by, designed, Gustave Eiffel)

→ _____ .

**2** 건물 안의 모든 불이 꺼졌다. (turned, all the lights, off, in the building, were)

→ _____ .

**3** 나는 낯선 사람에 의해 미행당하고 있다. (a stranger, being, by, followed, I am)

→ _____ .

**4** 실종된 아이가 경찰에 의해 발견되었다. (been, by, the missing child, found, has, the police)

→ _____ .

# UNIT 21 주의해야 할 수동태

정답 및 해설 p.31

↗ **CHECK UP**   괄호 안에서 알맞은 것을 고르세요.

**1** Kelly was (given / given to) a birthday gift by Tom.  `A-1`

**2** She was seen (enter / entering) John's house.  `B`

**3** We were made (clean / to clean) the classroom by the teacher.  `B`

**4** I'm worried (about / in) the midterm exams.  `C`

**5** The glass bottle is filled (of / with) water.  `C`

**A**   각 문장을 주어진 말로 시작하는 두 가지의 수동태 문장으로 바꿔 쓰세요.

**1** My boss gave me a bonus.

→ I _____ .

→ A bonus _____ .

**2** Charlie sent me the invitation.

→ I _____ .

→ The invitation _____ .

**B**   괄호 안의 말을 바르게 배열하여 수동태 문장을 완성하시오.

**1** (taught, was, English, a native speaker, by)

→ Jongsu _____ .

**2** (given, some flowers, was)

→ Clara _____ .

**3** (singing, was, a song, heard)

→ The little girl _____ .

**4** (was, Laura, made, by, his teeth, to brush)

→ Ralph _____ .

**C**  [보기]에서 알맞은 전치사를 하나씩 골라 빈칸을 채우세요.

[보기]    to        in        at        for        with

**1** She's interested _____ mathematics.

**2** The singer is known _____ his various talents.

**3** They were satisfied _____ dinner.

**4** The actor is known _____ lots of Japanese people.

**5** The audience was surprised _____ her performance.


**D**  괄호 안에서 어법상 적절하지 않은 하나를 고르세요.

**1** Anderson was (named / elected / seen) captain of the team.

**2** Becky was (heard / made / seen) playing the flute.

**3** She was (given / sent / received) a diamond ring.

**4** We're (interested / pleased / satisfied) with our new teacher.

**5** I was (told / made / let) to park my car across the street.


## WRITING PRACTICE

우리말과 일치하도록 괄호 안의 말을 이용하여 수동태 문장을 완성하세요.

**1** Evan은 챔피언십 트로피를 받았다. (award)

Evan _____ _____ the championship trophy.

**2** 이웃집 개가 짖는 소리가 들렸다. (hear, bark)

My neighbor's dog _____ _____ _____.

**3** Annie는 옷에 관심이 별로 없다. (interested)

Annie is _____ very _____ _____ clothes.

**4** 경찰은 그 용의자에 대해 아무런 정보도 받지 못했다. (give, any information)

The police were _____ _____ _____ _____ about the suspect.

# 실전 TEST 02 Unit 11-21

[1-2] 다음 중 밑줄 친 부분의 의미가 나머지와 <u>다른</u> 하나를 고르세요.

**1**
① <u>May</u> I come in?
② It <u>may</u> be true.
③ Anyone <u>may</u> use this computer.
④ I'm sorry, but you <u>may</u> not enter.
⑤ You <u>may</u> go home now.

**2**
① Jason can't meet us this evening. He <u>must</u> work late.
② I don't have much time. I <u>must</u> go soon.
③ Ted isn't at school today. He <u>must</u> be ill.
④ We <u>must</u> write to Grandmother. It's her birthday tomorrow.
⑤ Excuse me for a minute. I <u>must</u> make a phone call.

**3** 다음 밑줄 친 부분 중 어법상 옳지 <u>않은</u> 것을 고르세요.

① <u>Are you having</u> a good time?
② I <u>was having</u> a serious talk with Mom when you called me.
③ What <u>are we having</u> for lunch?
④ He <u>is having</u> a careful look at the digital camera.
⑤ I <u>am having</u> a new laptop.

**4** 다음 중 Dave의 상황을 가장 잘 나타낸 것을 고르세요.

> Dave: I'm sorry, but I'm leaving in ten minutes.

① Dave is going out now.
② Dave is going to leave soon.
③ Dave will stay for a long time.
④ Dave should have left sooner.
⑤ Dave wants to talk more.

**5** 다음 중 대화의 밑줄 친 부분이 의미하는 것으로 가장 알맞은 것을 고르세요.

> Tom: Sorry. I'm so late!
> Jane: What happened?
> Tom: It was my first time coming here, so I got lost.
> Jane: Then you should have asked someone for directions!
> Tom: You're right. <u>I should have.</u>

① Tom asked somebody for directions.
② Tom asked for directions but was rejected.
③ Tom doesn't want to ask for directions.
④ Tom didn't ask anybody for directions.
⑤ Jane already knew Tom would ask for directions.

서술형
**6** 다음 두 문장이 같은 뜻이 되도록 빈칸에 알맞은 조동사를 쓰세요.

> Let's have a race!
> = _____ we have a race?

**7** 다음 중 어법상 옳은 것을 고르세요.

① If it will snow tomorrow, we'll stay home.
② I'll help you when I will finish this work.
③ Do you know if he'll join us tonight?
④ I don't know when she calls me again.
⑤ Listen to my advice if you'll want to succeed.

서술형

**[8-9]** 다음 글을 한 문장으로 요약할 때, 빈칸에 알맞은 말을 쓰세요.

**8**

Yesterday I went to a zoo and saw elephants. It was the first time I had seen elephants, so I was excited. They were very impressive.

→ I _____ never _____ elephants before yesterday.

**9**

My sister and I are playing a game. The game will be over by 6 o'clock.

→ We _____ _____ finished playing the game by 6 o'clock.

**10** 다음 중 어법상 옳지 <u>않은</u> 것을 고르세요.

① An e-mail will be sent to her tomorrow.
② A trip to Russia is planning by Jimmy.
③ This suit has been designed by my wife.
④ Strict rules should be made to keep this school clean.
⑤ These boots were worn by many women last winter.

서술형

**11** 다음 그림과 일치하도록 괄호 안의 동사를 사용하여 문장을 완성하세요.

(30분 전)

↓

(현재)

She _____ _____ _____
for the bus for half an hour. (wait)

**12** 다음 문장을 수동태로 바꿀 때, 빈칸에 들어갈 알맞은 말을 고르세요.

My grandmother took care of me when I was young.

→ I _____
my grandmother when I was young.

① took care of by
② was taken care of
③ was took care of by
④ was taken care of by
⑤ was taken care by

13 ① Is Sammy going to visit Paris this winter?
  – Will Sammy visit Paris this winter?
② The news can't be true.
  – The news may not be true.
③ You don't have to do it now.
  – You don't need to do it now.
④ Can he repair the car?
  – Is he able to repair the car?
⑤ You should listen to your parents.
  – You ought to listen to your parents.

14 ① Jim can't have won the gold medal.
  – It's impossible that Jim won the gold medal.
② The police should have gathered more proof.
  – The police had to gather more proof.
③ She must have committed the robbery.
  – It's certain that she committed the robbery.
④ Peter may have stolen her money.
  – Perhaps Peter stole her money.
⑤ There used to be a garden here.
  – A garden that was here is gone.

**서술형**

15 다음 우리말과 일치하도록 괄호 안의 말을 바르게 배열하여 문장을 완성하세요.

> 부유해지고 싶다면, 그렇게 돈을 낭비하지 말아야 한다. (money, to, you, ought, waste, not)

→ If you want to be rich, _____
_____ like that.

16 다음은 어느 학급에서 주번이 해야 하는 일들입니다. 내용과 일치하지 <u>않는</u> 것을 고르세요.

- You must be in school by 8:30 in the morning.
- You don't have to clean the classroom after school.
- You need to clean the blackboard after every class.
- You don't need to empty the trash can after every class.
- You must not leave before your teacher tells you to.

① 방과 후 청소할 필요가 없다.
② 매 수업 후 칠판을 닦아야 한다.
③ 아침 8시 30분까지 등교해야 한다.
④ 교사의 허락 없이 하교해도 괜찮다.
⑤ 매 수업 후 쓰레기통을 비우지 않아도 된다.

17 다음 글을 읽고, 괄호 안에 들어갈 알맞은 말을 고르세요.

Not all lies are bad. Sometimes white lies help you keep a job or a friend. A few months ago, a friend asked me, "Do you like my new dress? I bought it yesterday." But I didn't like the dress, so I told her so. As a result, she refused to talk to me for a long time. In another case, I told my boss my opinion of him and his store. I told him the truth, but later I found out I had made a big mistake. I got fired! I _____ a white lie then!

① must tell
② must have told
③ may have told
④ should have told
⑤ shouldn't have told

**18** 다음 빈칸에 들어갈 말이 바르게 짝지어진 것을 고르세요.

Vincent van Gogh was born in the Netherlands in 1853. He was a religious man, so he worked as a preacher in England. Later, he ___ⓐ___ to become a painter, as he ___ⓑ___ by Millet. His younger brother, Theo, introduced him to *Impressionist painters. His brother was a remarkable man. Though he was poor himself, he always financed Vincent. In letters between the brothers, we can see that Vincent felt grateful for Theo's help.

*Impressionist 인상파의

|  | ⓐ | ⓑ |
|---|---|---|
| ① | decides | impressed |
| ② | decides | was impressed |
| ③ | decided | has impressed |
| ④ | decided | had been impressed |
| ⑤ | decides | has been impressed |

**19** 다음 중 시제가 어법상 옳지 않은 것을 고르세요.

① I drink orange juice after each meal.
② He is an engineer. He works for a big electrical company.
③ Chuseok falls in mid-September this year.
④ Genghis Khan conquers most of Asia in the 12th century.
⑤ Water turns into gas at 100 ˚C.

**20** 다음 중 밑줄 친 능동태를 수동태로, 수동태를 능동태로 바꾼 것이 적절하지 않은 것을 고르세요.

① Our daily lives have been changed significantly by smartphones. ② They are used by children, adults and even old people. It seems that ③ everybody has been affected by this new technology. ④ Smartphones are often used when we buy a book or order a sweater online. ⑤ Children use them for games. As this technology develops, our lives will become more dependent on it.

① Smartphones have changed our daily lives significantly.
② Children, adults and even old people use them.
③ This new technology has affected everybody.
④ We often use smartphones.
⑤ They are used by games for children.

**21** 다음 글을 한 문장으로 가장 적절하게 요약한 것을 고르세요.

Last year Bill went on a trip to Brazil. He liked the country so much that he decided to stay there. He didn't come back. That's why he is not here tonight.

① Bill went to Brazil.
② Bill is going to Brazil.
③ Bill has gone to Brazil.
④ Bill has been to Brazil.
⑤ Bill might have been to Brazil.

# UNIT 22 명사

↗ **CHECK UP**  괄호 안에서 알맞은 것을 고르세요.

**1** There are a lot of (book / books) on the shelf.  `B - 1`

**2** I'll have (milks / two glasses of milk), please.  `B - 3`

**3** Economics (is / are) my favorite subject.  `C - 1`

**4** Jimmy is wearing (sunglass / sunglasses).  `C - 2`

**5** He is kind and has (a good manner / good manners).  `C - 3`

**A**  그림과 일치하도록 주어진 말을 이용하여 문장을 완성하세요.

**1** cup, coffee

There are _____.

**2** glass, water

There are _____.

**3** piece, paper

There are _____.

**4** slice, bread

There are _____.

**B**  괄호 안에서 알맞은 것을 고르세요.

**1** Some shocking news (was / were) released last night.

**2** The police (is / are) running after the thief.

**3** Where (is my jean / are my jeans)?

**4** Statistics (is / are) a difficult subject for me.

**C** 괄호 안에서 어법상 적절하지 <u>않은</u> 하나를 고르세요.

**1** Do you have (stamp / any stamps / a few stamps)?

**2** While she was washing the dishes, she dropped (a glass / three glass / some glasses).

**3** He drinks (a cup of coffees / a glass of juice / a cup of tea) every morning.

**4** I ate (two eggs / porks / three bananas) for lunch.

**D** 어법상 <u>틀린</u> 부분을 고쳐 문장을 다시 쓰세요.

**1** Be careful when you use the scissor.

→ _____

**2** World peace are the most important thing.

→ _____

**3** My father works as a custom officer.

→ _____

**4** At least 90 peoples were killed in the attack.

→ _____

**5** I visited a Bangkok on a business trip.

→ _____

## WRITING PRACTICE

우리말과 일치하도록 괄호 안의 말을 이용하여 문장을 완성하세요.

**1** 나는 바지 두 벌을 샀다. (pair, pants)

I bought _____ _____ _____ _____.

**2** Edward는 오늘 와인을 세 잔 마셨다. (glass, wine)

Edward drank _____ _____ _____ _____ today.

**3** 그녀의 아기는 머리숱이 많다. (a lot of, hair)

Her baby _____ _____ _____ _____ _____.

↗ **CHECK UP**  괄호 안에서 알맞은 것을 고르세요.

**1** He's (a my old friend / an old friend of mine). `A·1`

**2** Arnold waited for you for (a / an) hour. `A·1`

**3** What is (a / the) fastest way to the airport? `B·2`

**4** I went to Jeju Island by (a plane / plane). `C`

**5** We played (the baseball / baseball) the other day. `C`


**A**  빈칸에 a 또는 an를 알맞게 쓰세요.

**1** Can you drive _____ car?

**2** I moved to _____ apartment last month.

**3** There is _____ woman behind you.

**4** Is there _____ university around here?

**5** Billy is _____ honest and kind man.

**6** It is _____ useful method to solve this problem.


**B**  빈칸에 the가 필요한 곳에는 the를 쓰고, 필요 없는 곳에는 × 표시하세요.

**1** It is _____ best movie I've ever seen.

**2** I go to _____ church with my family every Sunday.

**3** Erica is _____ only female student in the class.

**4** She went to Busan by _____ train.

**5** _____ moon is very bright tonight.

**6** My hobby is playing _____ flute.

**7** The engineers went to _____ hospital to fix its computer system.

**8** Greg used to live in _____ United Kingdom and now lives in _____ Canada.

**C** [보기]에서 알맞은 것을 골라 빈칸을 채우세요. (필요 없으면 × 표시 할 것)

[보기]　a　　an　　the

Dave is fifteen and a middle school student. He goes to school by (1) _____ subway. (2) _____ classrooms in (3) _____ school are small. He has six classes every day and each class lasts for (4) _____ hour. After (5) _____ school, he comes home and does homework. Then, he always eats (6) _____ dinner with his family at 7 p.m. He often plays (7) _____ basketball with his younger brother after dinner. After that, he usually goes to (8) _____ bed at around 10 p.m.

**D** 문장의 밑줄 친 부분을 바르게 고쳐 쓰세요.

**1** Nancy is holding <u>the her baby</u>.　　　　　　　　　　_____

**2** I go grocery shopping <u>once week</u>.　　　　　　　　_____

**3** This is <u>a biggest diamond</u> in the world.　　　　　_____

**4** <u>The dead</u> is not able to speak.　　　　　　　　　_____

**5** <u>Sandwiches I bought from the store</u> were cheap and delicious.　　　　　　　　　　　　　　　_____

---

**WRITING PRACTICE**

우리말과 일치하도록 괄호 안의 말을 이용하여 문장을 완성하세요.

**1** Cathy는 그의 딸이다. (a, daughter)

Cathy is _____ _____ of _____.

**2** 한국의 미래는 젊은이들에게 달려 있다. (depend on)

Korea's future _____ _____ _____ young.

**3** 이메일로 우리에게 연락하실 수 있습니다. (contact)

You can _____ _____ _____ e-mail.

↗ **CHECK UP** 괄호 안에서 알맞은 것을 고르세요.

**1** I bought (this / these) shoes in Laos. `B·1`

**2** Would you pass me (that / those) magazine? `B·2`

**3** Joseph sometimes talks to (himself / hisself). `C·1`

**4** They organized the party (themself / themselves). `C·2`

**5** He is eating lunch (with himself / by himself). `C·3`

**A** 그림과 일치하도록 this, these 또는 that, those를 알맞게 쓰세요.

**1**

_____ is my laptop computer.

**2**

_____ is John's motorcycle.

**3**

_____ are peaches.

**4**

_____ are her roses.

**5**

_____ is a microwave oven.

**6**

_____ are my dogs.

**B** 밑줄 친 부분이 가리키는 말을 영어로 쓰세요.

**1** Jessie takes the bus to work. <u>It</u> stops near her house. _____

**2** I take dance lessons every week. <u>They</u> are fun. _____

**3** The goods at this store are better than <u>those</u> at that store. _____

**4** A : Andrew seems to love Julia.

B : Why do you think <u>that</u>? _____

**C**     빈칸에 알맞은 재귀대명사를 써서 대화를 완성하세요.

**1**   A : Who made this wooden doghouse?

     B : My grandfather made it _____.

**2**   A : Who planned your trip?

     B : We _____ planned it.

**3**   A : Can you buy me this?

     B : No, you'll have to pay for it _____.


**D**     빈칸에 알맞은 재귀대명사를 쓰고, 그 역할을 [보기]에서 하나씩 골라 기호로 쓰세요.

[보기]   ⓐ 동사의 목적어     ⓑ 전치사의 목적어     ⓒ 주어 강조     ⓓ 목적어 강조

**1**   Take care of _____.            (역할) _____

**2**   I want to drive this car _____.      (역할) _____

**3**   He hurt _____ outside.         (역할) _____

**4**   I didn't like the actor, but I liked the movie _____.    (역할) _____


## WRITING PRACTICE

우리말과 일치하도록 괄호 안의 말을 바르게 배열하여 문장을 완성하세요.

**1**   너는 모든 것을 혼자 힘으로 할 수 있다. (everything, do, yourself, by)

    → You can _____.

**2**   나는 면도를 하는 동안 베었다. (cut, was, myself, I, shaving, while)

    → I _____.

**3**   그의 의견은 그의 아버지와는 달랐다. (from, different, his father, that of)

    → His opinion was _____.

# UNIT 25 it의 다양한 쓰임, one, another, other

정답 및 해설 p.38

### ☑ CHECK UP    괄호 안에서 알맞은 것을 고르세요.

**1** (Time / It) is a quarter to five.    `A·1`

**2** These bags are too expensive. Please show me some cheaper (one / ones).    `B·1`

**3** These are my favorite cookies. Can I have (another / other)?    `B·2`

**4** Some students like school uniforms. (Others / The other) don't.    `B·3`

**5** I have two sisters. One lives here and (another / the other) in Texas.    `B·3`


### A    [보기]에서 알맞은 말을 골라 빈칸을 채우세요.

[보기]    one        ones        it

**1** Simon likes apples but not green _____.

**2** I have a ticket for the concert. Do you have _____?

**3** Rachel lost her umbrella, so she bought a new _____.

**4** I lost my key but I soon found _____ under the sofa.

**5** I'm washing the dirty dishes, and she's drying the clean _____.


### B    [보기]에서 알맞은 말을 하나씩 골라 빈칸을 채우세요.

[보기]    another    other    the other    others    the others    one another

**1** Some of the eggs went bad. _____ were fine.

**2** If you love each other, respect _____.

**3** We saw two movies. One was exciting, but _____ was boring.

**4** Do you have any _____ questions before I answer?

**5** Baseball is one popular sport in the US. _____ are basketball and football.

**6** I liked the shirt a lot, so I bought _____ shirt just like it.

**64**    G-ZONE WORKBOOK

**C** 괄호 안에서 알맞은 것을 고르세요.

**1** I visited two European countries where people speak French.

One was France, and (the other / the others) was Switzerland.

**2** There are four necklaces to choose from.

Two are expensive, but (the other / the others) are not.

**3** (Some / Others) students live with their parents.

(Others / The others) live on campus. Still others live in apartments near the campus.

**D** 우리말과 일치하도록 빈칸에 알맞은 말을 쓰세요.

**1** 그가 이곳을 떠난다는 것은 사실이다.

_____ is true that he will leave here.

**2** 난 네 시계가 마음에 들어! 넌 그것을 어디에서 샀니?

I like your watch! Where did you buy _____?

**3** 차 한 잔 더 하시겠어요?

Would you like _____ cup of tea?

**4** 나는 친구들에게 몇 장의 카드를 썼다. 하나는 분홍색이고, 나머지는 연한 파란색이다.

I wrote some cards for friends. _____ is pink and the others are light blue.

## WRITING PRACTICE

우리말과 일치하도록 괄호 안의 말을 바르게 배열하여 문장을 완성하세요.

**1** 역사로부터 배우는 것은 중요하다. (is, important, it, to learn)

→ _____ from history.

**2** John은 한 손에는 머그잔을, 다른 한 손에는 책을 들고 있었다. (the, a book, other, and, one hand, in)

→ John was holding a mug in _____.

**3** 객관식 문제에는 보통 다섯 개의 선택지가 있다. 그중 하나는 정답이고 나머지는 오답이다.

(the others, a correct answer, are, not, and, is)

→ There are usually five choices in a multiple choice question.

One of them _____.

# UNIT 26 그 외 대명사의 여러 쓰임

정답 및 해설 p.40

☑ **CHECK UP** 괄호 안에서 알맞은 것을 고르세요.

**1** I couldn't see (anything / something) in the dark.　　　A - 2

**2** Each of the kids (is / are) lovable and precious.　　　B - 2

**3** (None / No) of the stories are true.　　　B - 3

**4** (Both / Neither) of the twins is blond.　　　C - 2

**5** (Either / Neither) restaurant is fine with me. The both serve good food.　　　C - 3

---

**A** 우리말과 일치하도록 빈칸에 알맞은 말을 쓰세요.

**1** 그 반의 모든 아이가 시험을 통과했다.

＿＿＿＿＿＿ child in the class passed the exam.

**2** 남은 표가 전혀 없다.

There are ＿＿＿＿＿＿ tickets left.

**3** 그들 중 아무도 어젯밤 그 파티에 오지 않았다.

＿＿＿＿＿＿ of them came to the party last night.

**4** 모든 상점이 문을 닫았다.

＿＿＿＿＿＿ the stores are closed.

---

**B** [보기]에서 알맞은 말을 골라 빈칸을 채우세요.

[보기]　not any　　neither　　either

**1** Both of the dresses are on sale now.

You can buy ＿＿＿＿＿＿＿ of the dresses for 20 dollars.

**2** There is no one who knows the answer.

So there are ＿＿＿＿＿＿＿ students who can answer the question.

**3** I have appointments on Friday and Sunday.

＿＿＿＿＿＿＿ of the days is okay with me. How about Saturday?

**C**    어법상 <u>틀린</u> 부분을 고쳐 문장을 다시 쓰세요.

**1** Every bottle are filled with water.

→ _____

**2** Both of the four men are Irish.

→ _____

**3** I thought I heard anyone at the door.

→ _____

**4** Does someone know the words to this song?

→ _____

**5** Each of the players were able to score points.

→ _____

**6** All these children is special.

→ _____

## WRITING PRACTICE

우리말과 일치하도록 [보기]와 괄호 안의 말을 이용하여 문장을 완성하세요.

[보기]    all        any        every        neither

**1** 그것은 매우 간단한 문제이다. 어떤 바보라도 그것을 풀 수 있다. (fool, solve)

It's a very simple question. _____ _____ _____ _____ it.

**2** 나는 두 개의 펜이 있었는데, 그중 아무것도 써지지 않았다. (them, work)

I had two pens, but _____ _____ _____ _____.

**3** 이 호텔의 모든 방에는 노트북 컴퓨터가 있다. (have)

_____ room in this hotel _____ a laptop computer.

**4** 4세 이상의 모든 어린이는 입장권이 필요합니다. (need)

_____ children over 4 years of age _____ a ticket.

↗ **CHECK UP** 괄호 안에서 알맞은 것을 고르세요.

**1** I want to eat (sweet something / something sweet).　A-1

**2** Look at those (sleeping / asleep) puppies.　A-2

**3** Carlos is a warm and (friendly / friendless) man.　B

**4** There aren't (many / much) houses around here.　C-1

**5** I spent (a little / a few) time in the park.　C-2

**A** 밑줄 친 부분의 뜻을 각각 우리말로 쓰세요.

**1** ⓐ At the <u>present</u> time, we have no choice.

_____

　ⓑ All the members were <u>present</u> at the meeting.

_____

**2** ⓐ This bag is very <u>light</u>. A child could carry it.

_____

　ⓑ The room is <u>light</u> and warm.

_____

**3** ⓐ Is this the <u>right</u> way to the subway station?

_____

　ⓑ He felt severe pain in his <u>right</u> shoulder.

_____

**B** 빈칸에 many 또는 much를 알맞게 쓰세요.

**1** I don't have _____ work to do today.

**2** He sang _____ songs for his children.

**3** How _____ money do I need to buy it?

**4** I think that our teacher gives us too _____ homework.

**5** Don't eat too _____ sugar. It's not good for your health.

**6** Amber has traveled to _____ countries, including India and South Africa.

**C**     **[보기]에서 알맞은 말을 골라 빈칸을 채우세요.**

> [보기]    a few      few      a little      little

**1**   I'm thirsty. Can you give me _____ water, please?

**2**   There is _____ food left. Let's go grocery shopping.

**3**   I don't have a job at the moment, so I have _____ money.

**4**   My car is very old, but I have had _____ problems with it.

**5**   This box is too heavy. Can you give me _____ help?

**6**   We need _____ tomatoes for this sauce. Can you bring me some from the fridge?

**D**     **문장의 밑줄 친 부분을 바르게 고쳐 쓰세요.**

**1**   Wow, he's holding an alive snake!      _____

**2**   Let's eat spicy something for lunch today.      _____

**3**   He drove a little kilometers to a small village.      _____

**4**   I have a few friends, so I always feel lonely.      _____

**5**   We have lot of things to prepare before going camping.      _____

---

### WRITING PRACTICE

괄호 안의 말을 써서 다음 [조건]에 맞는 문장을 완성하세요.

> [조건]    주어진 명사를 우리말에 맞는 형용사로 바꿀 것

**1**   그녀는 희망에 찬 미소로 그를 바라보았다. (hope)

    She looked at him with a _____ _____.

**2**   아, 죄송합니다. 제가 어리석은 실수를 했어요. (fool)

    Oh, I'm sorry. I made a _____ _____.

**3**   너무 많은 에너지 드링크를 마시는 것은 아이들에게 위험할 수도 있다. (danger)

    It can _____ _____ for children to drink too many energy drinks.

# UNIT 28 부사

정답 및 해설 p.42

**☑ CHECK UP** 괄호 안에서 알맞은 것을 고르세요.

**1** Bart was waiting (patient / patiently) for Gill. `A - 1`

**2** She speaks French very (good / well). `A - 3`

**3** He tried very (hard / hardly) to remember her name. `B - 3`

**4** I (always will / will always) love you. `C - 1`

**5** I'll pick (you up / up you) at the airport. `C - 2`

---

**A** 두 문장이 같은 뜻이 되도록 빈칸에 알맞은 말을 쓰세요.

**1** Carl is a good cook.

= Carl cooks _____.

**2** Dave is a crazy driver.

= Dave drives _____.

**3** Alex is a slow walker.

= Alex walks _____.

**4** Barbara is a fast runner.

= Barbara runs _____.

---

**B** 괄호 안의 말을 바르게 배열하여 문장을 완성하세요.

**1** (early, wake, never, up)

→ I _____.

**2** (always, must, a seat belt, wear)

→ You _____.

**3** (often, closed, are, on Sundays)

→ Stores _____.

**4** (home, leaves, usually, at 7:00)

→ My father _____.

**C** 문장의 밑줄 친 부분을 바르게 고쳐 쓰세요.

**1** I lost my wallet, so I'm <u>looking it for</u>. _____

**2** The light is too bright. Can you <u>turn off it</u>? _____

**3** The new worker <u>always will do</u> his best for the company. _____

**4** Take your umbrella with you. <u>It's raining heavy outside</u>. _____

**5** My husband and I <u>work very hardly</u> from Monday to Friday. _____


**D** 밑줄 친 부분이 형용사인지 부사인지 구분하여 같은 품사끼리 그 번호를 쓰세요.

**1** I can't jump that <u>high</u>.

**2** Do you like shoes with <u>high</u> heels?

**3** I can <u>hardly</u> believe my eyes.

**4** I hate to sit on that <u>hard</u> wooden chair.

**5** He had thought <u>hard</u> before starting the business.

**6** My younger brother always gets up <u>late</u>.

**7** We arrived at the resort in the <u>late</u> afternoon.

**8** Look at that <u>lovely</u> wedding dress the bride is wearing!

• 형용사: _____     • 부사: _____


---

**WRITING PRACTICE**

우리말과 일치하도록 괄호 안의 말을 바르게 배열하여 문장을 완성하세요.

**1** 나는 보통 밤 11시에 잔다. (at 11 p.m., I, go to bed, usually)

→ _____.

**2** 그것을 끄든지 소리를 줄이든지 해라. (it, turn, or, down, turn, off, it)

→ _____.

**3** 나는 그 셔츠를 입었다가 즉시 그것을 벗었다. (and then, the shirt, took, on, it, put, off)

→ I _____ at once.

# UNIT **29** 비교 I

정답 및 해설 p.43

↗ **CHECK UP**   **괄호 안에서 알맞은 것을 고르세요.**

**1** This problem is (difficulter / more difficult) than that one.  `A-1`

**2** Today is the (most bad / worst) day of my life.  `A-2`

**3** Juyeong kicked the ball (farer / farther) than Jisung.  `A-2`

**4** Matt is (very / much) more famous than his father.  `B-2`

**5** The more we have, the (more / most) we want.  `C-1`

---

**A**   **예시와 같이 그림과 일치하도록 괄호 안의 말을 알맞은 형태로 바꾸어 빈칸을 완성하세요.**

**0**

Mike is <u>taller than</u> Jake. (tall)

**1**

A motorcycle goes _____ a bicycle. (fast)

**2**

Drums sound _____ a guitar. (loud)

**3**

This restaurant's food is_____ that one's. (delicious)

**밑줄 친 말의 비교급과 최상급을 [보기]에서 찾아 쓰세요.**

[보기]    less       farther      more       further      better

         least      farthest     most       furthest     best

|  | 비교급 | 최상급 |
|---|---|---|
| **1** The school is nearby but the library is <u>far</u>. | _____ | _____ |
| **2** I just need a <u>little</u> time and money. | _____ | _____ |
| **3** He loved her very <u>much</u>. | _____ | _____ |

**C**

**어법상 틀린 부분을 고쳐 문장을 다시 쓰세요.**

**1** Your kite is flying high than mine.

→ _____

**2** Math is very easier than English.

→ _____

**3** The more you eat, the much weight you gain.

→ _____

**4** It's July, and the weather is getting hoter and hoter.

→ _____

## WRITING PRACTICE

우리말과 일치하도록 괄호 안의 말을 알맞은 형태로 바꾸어 문장을 완성하세요.

**1** 그 신형 차는 기존 모델보다 연료를 덜 사용한다. (fuel)

The new car uses _____ _____ _____ earlier models.

**2** 시험이 어려울수록 더 많이 배운다. (hard, much)

_____ _____ the test is, _____ _____ you learn.

**3** 석유 가격이 점점 더 높아지고 있다. (get, high)

The price of oil is _____ _____ _____ _____ .

**4** 그녀는 그보다 덜 아름답게 노래 부른다. (beautifully)

She sings _____ _____ _____ him.

☑ CHECK UP  괄호 안에서 알맞은 것을 고르세요.

**1** Mary is as (old / older) as Jane.   `A-1`

**2** Susan walked as quietly as (possible / possibly).   `A-3`

**3** Glen runs the (faster / fastest) of us all.   `B-1`

**4** He is the (greater / greatest) artist I've ever met.   `C-1`

**5** This is one of the best (restaurant / restaurants) in this city.   `C-2`

**A** 주어진 문장이 모두 같은 뜻이 되도록 [보기]에서 알맞은 말을 골라 빈칸을 채우세요.

[보기]   as   students   more   most   student

**1** Tanya is the _____ talkative student in the class.

**2** No student in the class is _____ talkative as Tanya.

**3** No student in the class is _____ talkative than Tanya.

**4** Tanya is more talkative than any other _____ in the class.

**5** Tanya is more talkative than all the other _____ in the class.

**B** 어법상 틀린 부분을 고쳐 문장을 다시 쓰세요.

**1** She works as hardly as possible.

→ _____

**2** Your room is as twice big as mine.

→ _____

**3** That is more difficult exam I've ever taken.

→ _____

**4** This is one of the best product of our company.

→ _____

## C  문장이 같은 뜻이 되도록 빈칸에 알맞은 말을 쓰세요.

**1** The novel is more interesting than the movie.

= The movie _____ as the novel.

**2** The ring is less valuable than the necklace.

= The ring is not _____ .

**3** Venice is the most beautiful city in the world.

= _____ more beautiful than Venice.

= No city in the world is as _____ .

= Venice is more _____ city in the world.

**4** Antarctica is the coldest place in the world.

= _____ is colder than Antarctica.

= No place in the world is as _____ .

= Antarctica is colder _____ places in the world.

## WRITING PRACTICE

괄호 안의 말을 써서 다음 [조건]에 맞는 문장을 완성하세요.

[조건]  「as + 원급 + as」 비교 표현을 사용할 것

**1** Ben은 Andy보다 나이가 세 배 많다. (old)

Ben is _____ _____ _____ _____ _____ Andy.

**2** 겨울의 낮은 여름의 낮만큼 길지 않다. (long)

Days in winter are _____ _____ _____ those in summer.

**3** 가능한 한 오래 숨을 참고 있어라. (long)

Hold your breath for _____ _____ _____ _____ .

= Hold your breath for _____ _____ _____ you _____ .

# UNIT 31 장소를 나타내는 전치사

↗ **CHECK UP**   괄호 안에서 알맞은 것을 고르세요.

**1** Jerry sat in front of (I / me).　　　　　　　　　　　　　A

**2** Tony fell (at / in) the river by accident.　　　　　　　　B

**3** The teacher sat (at / on) the chair.　　　　　　　　　　B

**4** This is the tallest building (in / at) the city.　　　　　C-2

**5** He put cheese (between / among) two slices of bread.　C-4

---

**A**   그림과 일치하도록 [보기]에서 알맞은 전치사를 하나씩 골라 빈칸을 채우세요.

[보기]　in front of　　under　　beside　　behind　　between　　on

**1** The computer is _____ the table.

**2** The monitor and the keyboard are _____ the table.

**3** The cat is _____ the monitor.

**4** The cat is _____ the monitor and the keyboard.

**5** The picture is _____ the monitor.

**6** The books are _____ the table.

---

**B**   우리말과 일치하도록 [보기]에서 알맞은 전치사를 하나씩 골라 빈칸을 채우세요.

[보기]　along　　to　　through　　among　　from

**1** Katie는 뉴욕에서 캘리포니아까지 기차로 여행했다.

Katie traveled _____ New York _____ California by train.

**2** 해변을 따라서 조깅하러 가자!

Let's go jogging _____ the beach.

**3** 큰 무리의 소 사이에 양 한 마리가 있다.

There is one sheep _____ the large group of cows.

**4** 이 문을 통과해서 가면, 거실이 보일 겁니다.

Go _____ this door, and you'll see the living room.


**C** 문장의 밑줄 친 부분을 바르게 고쳐 쓰세요.

**1** Who's that man behind she? _____

**2** There are tulips among the garden. _____

**3** Don't sit over the bench. It's wet. _____

**4** There are a lot of fish on this river. _____

**5** Their names are on the bottom of the list. _____


## WRITING PRACTICE

우리말과 일치하도록 각 상자 속 어구를 하나씩 연결하여 문장을 완성하세요.

| There's | often takes a walk | around | the ceiling |
| Monica | walked | across | the museum |
| We | a butterfly | on | the bridge carefully |

**1** 우리는 조심스럽게 그 다리를 가로질러 걸어갔다.

→ _____.

**2** 천장에 나비가 붙어 있다.

→ _____.

**3** Monica는 자주 박물관 주위를 산책한다.

→ _____.

⬈ **CHECK UP** **괄호 안에서 알맞은 것을 고르세요.**

**1** We're going to go out for dinner (at / on) Friday night. `A-1`

**2** Please take care of my son. I'll be back (in / at) 15 minutes. `A-2`

**3** I studied (by / until) midnight and went to bed. `B-1`

**4** The player has been playing soccer (from / since) 2005. `B-2`

**5** They've been working on the project (for / during) 7 months. `B-3`

**A** **[보기]에서 알맞은 말을 골라 빈칸을 채우세요.**

[보기]    in        at        on

**1** I went to sleep _____ 11 o'clock.

**2** It's four o'clock _____ the afternoon.

**3** I have a test _____ Monday morning.

**4** My friend and I went fishing _____ night.

**5** Kelly and her family went to Cuba _____ 2006.

**6** Aloha and Bruno used to go hiking _____ the spring.

**B** **의미상 가장 알맞은 것끼리 짝지어 문장을 완성하세요.**

**1** They have known each other          •          • (a) since they were young.

**2** He'll be away from Christmas Eve    •          • (b) until the end of the month.

**3** This job should be done              •          • (c) during her trip to Europe.

**4** She gave birth to a baby girl        •          • (d) by next Monday.

**C** 괄호 안에서 어법상 적절하지 <u>않은</u> 하나를 고르세요.

**1** Did you get a new job (after / on / in) April?

**2** I have to get to work (by / before / from) 9 a.m.

**3** He will be in Amsterdam (by / for / in) three days.

**4** Bob and Cindy met (during / since / after) the dance party.

**5** I mailed the letter today, and you will receive it (until / by / on) Monday.

**D** 어법상 <u>틀린</u> 부분을 고쳐 문장을 다시 쓰세요.

**1** The train arrives on 8 a.m.

→ _____

**2** I had to finish reading the whole book until Friday.

→ _____

**3** My parents have been married in 1995.

→ _____

**4** Erin waited for Sue in an hour and a half.

→ _____

---

## WRITING PRACTICE

우리말과 일치하도록 [보기]와 괄호 안의 말을 이용하여 문장을 완성하세요.

[보기]   by        until        in

**1** 내가 1, 2분 후에 거기로 갈게. (be there)

I'll _____ _____ _____ a minute or two.

**2** 나는 그 경기를 끝까지 지켜보았다. (the end)

I watched the game _____ _____ _____.

**3** 그 보고서는 이번 주 금요일까지 준비되어야 한다. (be ready)

The report needs to _____ _____ _____ _____ _____.

↗ **CHECK UP** 괄호 안에서 알맞은 것을 고르세요.

**1** Her father is suffering (of / from) heart disease. `A - 1`

**2** They asked me (for / against) information about the camp. `A - 2`

**3** Can I pay for the room (with / by) credit card? `B - 1`

**4** How do you say "sorry" (by / in) Japanese? `B - 1`

**5** This dress is made (from / of) silk. `B - 2`

**A** [보기]에서 알맞은 말을 골라 빈칸을 채우세요.

[보기]  by  with  in

**1** I want to dance _____ you.

**2** Willy usually goes to work _____ car.

**3** We had a discussion _____ English.

**4** You can eat the food _____ chopsticks or a spoon.

**5** You can turn off the computer _____ pressing this button.

**B** 우리말과 일치하도록 괄호 안의 말을 바르게 배열하여 문장을 완성하세요.

**1** 이 동전들은 구리로 만들어졌다. (made, these coins, of, copper, are)

→ _____ .

**2** Ron은 망치로 못을 내리쳤다. (with, hit, Ron, a hammer, a nail)

→ _____ .

**3** 그녀는 이집트의 문화에 대한 강연을 했다. (the culture of Egypt, she, on, gave a lecture)

→ _____ .

**4** Luke는 내가 그에게 조언해 준 것에 대해 고마워했다. (thanked, Luke, me, giving, for)

→ _____ him advice.

**C** 두 문장의 빈칸에 공통으로 들어갈 전치사를 쓰세요.

**1** I washed my hands _____ soap and water before lunch.

Gemma usually spends time _____ her friends on Friday nights.

**2** I sent my résumé _____ e-mail.

Jessie explained it _____ giving examples.

**3** Dorothy felt sorry _____ lying to her mother.

Did you vote _____ him?

**4** The British actor died _____ cancer.

This beautiful bag is made _____ old jeans.

**5** I went to the supermarket _____ foot.

We had a discussion _____ human rights.

**D** 괄호 안에서 알맞은 전치사를 고르세요.

**1** Our freshly baked bread is made (of / by) hand.

**2** The table is made (from / of) wood.

**3** She caught a dragonfly (with / by) a net.

**4** You can save money (by / for) using coupons.

**5** I always stay here when I am in London (about / on) business.

## WRITING PRACTICE

우리말과 일치하도록 [보기]와 괄호 안의 말을 이용하여 문장을 완성하세요.

[보기]   by   with   against

**1** 여기에 주차하는 것은 법에 어긋난다. (the law)

It's _____ _____ _____ to park here.

**2** Helen은 전화로 그 표를 예약했다. (reserve)

Helen _____ _____ _____ _____ phone.

**3** 그의 눈은 기쁨으로 반짝거리고 있었다. (shine, joy)

His eyes _____ _____ _____ _____.

# 실전 TEST 03  Unit 22-33

**1** 다음 중 짝지어진 두 단어의 관계가 나머지와 <u>다른</u> 하나를 고르세요.

① slow – slowly
② heavy – heavily
③ friend – friendly
④ honest – honestly
⑤ fortunate – fortunately

서술형

**2** 다음 두 문장이 같은 뜻이 되도록 빈칸을 완성하세요.

> I think a rose is the prettiest flower.
> = I think no flower is as _____
> _____ a rose.

**3** 다음 밑줄 친 부분 중 생략할 수 있는 것을 고르세요.

① Did you enjoy <u>yourself</u> at the party?
② Between <u>ourselves</u>, I really don't like him.
③ History repeats <u>itself</u>.
④ I wrote this book <u>myself</u>.
⑤ He lives in that house by <u>himself</u>.

**4** 다음 중 밑줄 친 단어의 쓰임이 적절하지 <u>않은</u> 것을 고르세요.

① Choose the right answer <u>among</u> A and B.
② They got <u>off</u> the bus immediately.
③ We walked <u>along</u> the street.
④ Did you come to Helsinki <u>on</u> business?
⑤ We went <u>through</u> a tough time together.

**5** 다음 빈칸에 들어갈 말이 바르게 짝지어진 것을 고르세요.

> • It was a useful _____ of information.
> • He gave me three _____ of socks for my birthday.
> • I need a _____ of paper to write on.

① sheet – piece – slice
② sheet – pieces – slice
③ piece – pair – piece
④ piece – pairs – sheet
⑤ piece – pairs – sheets

**6** 다음 중 [보기]와 뜻이 같은 문장을 고르세요.

> [보기]  Patience is the most important thing.

① Nothing is less important than patience.
② Nothing is as important as patience.
③ Anything is more important than patience.
④ Everything is as important as patience.
⑤ Patience is more important than nothing.

서술형

**7** 다음 빈칸에 공통으로 들어갈 알맞은 말을 쓰세요.

> • He goes to work _____ bus.
> • Make sure you're back _____ 12 o'clock.
> • Were you surprised _____ the news?

**8** 다음 중 어법상 옳은 것을 고르세요.

① I don't have some pens.
② He was originally against my idea.
③ She suffers by headaches.
④ Lucy made her own dress in a pair of scissors.
⑤ Red wine is made in grapes.

서술형

**9** 다음 우리말과 일치하도록 괄호 안의 말을 이용하여 문장을 완성하세요.

> 날씨가 따뜻해질수록 나는 기분이 더 좋아진다.
> (warm, good)

→ _____ _____ it gets,
_____ _____ I feel.

**10** 다음 중 짝지어진 두 문장의 뜻이 서로 다른 것을 고르세요.

① He tried to eat as little as possible.
  – He tried to eat as little as he could.
② He made the table for him.
  – He made the table himself.
③ I like neither of the ideas.
  – I don't like either of the ideas.
④ I have no nice dresses.
  – I don't have any nice dresses.
⑤ On the whole, Linda lived a happy life.
  – On the whole, Linda lived happily.

**11** 다음 중 [보기]의 밑줄 친 단어와 품사가 같은 것을 모두 고르세요. (2개)

> [보기]  I stayed at my aunt's during the holidays.

① Do you want to take a break?
② Martin put his coat on and left.
③ A necklace hung around her neck.
④ Have you seen this before?
⑤ I was looking for this notebook.

**12** 다음 빈칸에 공통으로 들어갈 알맞은 말을 고르세요.

- Thanks _____ your advice. It was very helpful.
- I'm so sorry _____ being late. My car had a problem on the way.

① by        ② from        ③ to
④ for        ⑤ until

**13** 다음 중 뜻이 나머지와 다른 하나를 고르세요.

① She is the smartest student in my class.
② She is smarter than any other student in my class.
③ No student in my class is as smart as her.
④ No student in my class is less smart than her.
⑤ No student in my class is smarter than her.

**14** 다음 밑줄 친 부분 중 어법상 옳지 <u>않은</u> 것을 고르세요

① The police <u>are looking for</u> witnesses.
② People often <u>says</u> we get three chances in life.
③ A glass of water every morning <u>is</u> good for your health.
④ Economics <u>is</u> a subject related to economy and finance.
⑤ Two cups of coffee <u>are</u> ready for you.

**15** 다음 중 [보기]의 It과 같은 용법으로 쓰인 것을 고르세요.

[보기]   Let's go home. <u>It</u> is getting dark.

① <u>It</u> is really easy to solve the problems.
② What day is <u>it</u> today?
③ She brought an umbrella but left <u>it</u> on the bus on the way.
④ <u>It</u> is important to read many books.
⑤ Don't do <u>it</u> again.

서술형

**16** 다음 글을 읽고, 밑줄 친 대명사가 가리키는 것을 본문에서 찾아 영어로 쓰세요.

I was invited to Linda's birthday party. (1) <u>She</u> turned sixteen, so her father threw a big party for her. (2) <u>It</u> was held in a fancy Chinese restaurant. Everyone at the party enjoyed the food a lot. I think (3) <u>that</u> was the most delicious food I've ever had.

(1) _____ (1단어)
(2) _____ (3단어)
(3) _____ (2단어)

서술형

**17** 다음 밑줄 친 부분 중 어법상 옳지 <u>않은</u> 것을 모두 바르게 고쳐 쓰세요. (2개)

Hollywood has made interesting movies about Dracula. In them, he always searches for ⓐ <u>warm something</u> to drink — blood! But Vlad Dracul, ⓑ <u>the real Dracula</u>, never drank blood. He was indeed ⓒ <u>a cruel man</u>, though. He killed ⓓ <u>much people</u> in his Romanian castle in the 1400s. Fortunately, the castle was well maintained over the years. And ⓔ <u>the present owners</u> of Dracular's castle now allow tourists to visit.

(1) _____ → _____
(2) _____ → _____

서술형

**18** 다음 빈칸에 a, an, the 중 알맞은 것을 쓰세요.

A: Hello. I'd like to speak to the landlord, please.
B: I'm the manager of the building. Can I help you?
A: I'm looking for (1) _____ new apartment. Are there any small apartments for rent in your building?
B: Yes, there's one on the third floor.
A: How many bedrooms are there?
B: Just one. And there is a kitchen and a living room.
A: When can I see (2) _____ apartment?
B: How about tomorrow at 9 a.m.?

**19**  ① Let's go to have a lunch.

② It's 10. Time to go to bed, kids!

③ He used to play basketball in high school.

④ The clerk was busy talking to another customer.

⑤ There are several hairs on the floor. You should pick them up.

**20**  ① He never does his homework before dinner.

② The rich have to help the poor.

③ Both of us were excited to hear the news.

④ She was satisfied with herself.

⑤ Tomorrow will be very hotter than today.

**21**  다음 밑줄 친 부분 중 어법상 옳지 <u>않은</u> 것을 고르세요.

Why do some people ① <u>pay more</u> for car insurance than others? Insurance companies calculate your rate based on the risk. For example, insurance rates of married men are lower than those of unmarried men. Statistics show that married men have ② <u>fewer</u> accidents. Another factor is the number of miles you drive each year. The more you drive, ③ <u>the most possibilities</u> of accidents there are. As a result, you pay more. Another kind of insurance protects your car. A more expensive car costs more to insure than ④ <u>a less expensive one</u>. Sports cars have the highest rate of theft, and owners of these cars ⑤ <u>pay the most</u>.

①          ②          ③          ④          ⑤

**[22–23]** 다음 글을 읽고, 물음에 답하세요.

Arthur Koestler was a Hungarian-British author ____ⓐ____ novels and essays. He was one ____ⓐ____ the most important writers of the 20th century. He was born in Budapest ____ⓑ____ 1905. His early career was in journalism. At the age of 35, he published his most famous novel, *Darkness at Noon*, which brought him global fame. For the next forty-three years he lived ____ⓑ____ the UK and wrote novels, biographies, and numerous essays about many things.

**22**  위 글의 빈칸 ⓐ에 공통으로 들어갈 알맞은 말을 고르세요.

① by          ② from          ③ to
④ for          ⑤ of

**23**  위 글의 빈칸 ⓑ에 공통으로 들어갈 알맞은 말을 고르세요.

① by          ② in          ③ to
④ for          ⑤ from

서술형
**24**  다음 우리말과 일치하도록 빈칸에 알맞은 말을 쓰세요.

> 서울에서 홍콩까지 가는 데 비행기로 4시간 걸린다.

→ It takes four hours by airplane to go _____ Seoul _____ Hong Kong.

↗ **CHECK UP** 괄호 안에서 알맞은 것을 고르세요.

**1** My father promised (to don't / not to) smoke again. `A`

**2** (It's / That's) not difficult to cook chicken curry. `C-1`

**3** The kid refused (eat / to eat) anything. `C-2`

**4** His dream is (to travel / travel) all over the world. `C-3`

**5** I don't know (how / how I) to do it without you. `C-4`

**A** [보기]에서 알맞은 말을 골라 to부정사 형태로 바꾸어 빈칸을 완성하세요.

[보기]   write   go   visit   take   do

**1** Dan hates _____ his homework.

**2** You need _____ this medicine three times a day.

**3** I'm planning _____ to Europe on vacation.

**4** I'd like _____ Hong Kong someday.

**5** My job is _____ songs.

**B** 두 문장이 같은 뜻이 되도록 빈칸에 알맞은 말을 쓰세요.

**1** To work out every day is my goal.

= It _____ _____ _____ _____ work out every day.

**2** I'll decide later what I should say.

= I'll decide later _____ _____ _____.

**3** Show me the way to the bus stop, please.

= Show me _____ _____ get to the bus stop, please.

**4** Tell me where I should go to learn more about photography.

= Tell me _____ _____ _____ to learn more about photography.

## C

괄호 안의 말을 바르게 배열하여 문장을 완성하세요.

**1** (not, go, decided, to the baseball game, to)

→ We _____ .

**2** (to, wants, a successful diplomat, be)

→ Jessie _____ .

**3** (fun, to, comic books, read, is)

→ It _____ .

**4** (play, likes, computer games, to)

→ Richard _____ .


## D

밑줄 친 to부정사(구)의 역할을 [보기]에서 골라 쓰세요.

[보기]   주어        목적어        보어

**1** Her boyfriend likes to drive.               _____

**2** We want to invite you to our wedding.       _____

**3** It is important to love yourself.           _____

**4** He wants us to go fishing with him.         _____

**5** Her role is to help people achieve their goals.   _____


## WRITING PRACTICE

우리말과 일치하도록 [보기]의 의문사와 괄호 안의 동사를 이용하여 문장을 완성하세요.

[보기]   what      how      where

**1** 어디에서 만날지 제게 문자를 보내주세요. (meet)

Please text me _____ _____ _____ you.

**2** 점심으로 무엇을 먹을지 결정했니? (have)

Have you decided _____ _____ _____ for lunch?

**3** 그 게임을 어떻게 하는지 보여 줄래? (play)

Can you show me _____ _____ _____ _____ _____ ?

# UNIT 35 형용사·부사처럼 쓰이는 to부정사

정답 및 해설 p.53

⤴ **CHECK UP** 괄호 안에서 알맞은 것을 고르세요.

**1** I need a cushion to (sit / sit on).　　　　　　　　　　　　A-1

**2** Try to eat healthy food in order (not to / to not) get sick.　B-1

**3** I turned on the TV (and find / to find) I had become a superstar.　B-2

**4** Brian was glad (to see / saw) his old friend again.　　　　B-4

**5** (To be / I am) honest with you, he is not a good man.　　B-5

**A** 괄호 안의 말을 바르게 배열하여 문장을 완성하세요.

**1** (to, say, strange)

→ _____, I don't feel any pain.

**2** (no money, has, spend, to)

→ He _____.

**3** (a pencil, with, to, draw)

→ I need _____.

**4** (hard, are, to, find)

→ Good books _____.

**5** (to, a good movie, is, see, this)

→ _____ with your whole family.

**B** [보기]에서 알맞은 말을 골라 빈칸을 채우세요.

[보기]　to begin with　　to make matters worse　　to be frank

**1** I lost my job. _____, I broke up with my boyfriend.

**2** I can't recommend the movie. _____, I didn't like it.

**3** He has many good points. _____, he is very friendly.

**C** 두 문장이 같은 뜻이 되도록 빈칸에 알맞은 말을 쓰세요.

**1** If you saw him play soccer, you'd think that he was a pro.

= _____ _____ him play soccer, you'd think that he was a pro.

**2** She tried to speak, but cried instead.

= She tried to speak, only _____ _____ instead.

**3** We read the movie review and were excited.

= We were _____ _____ _____ the movie review.

**4** He checked his email so as to see the schedule.

= He checked his email _____ _____ _____ see the schedule.


**D** 괄호 안에서 밑줄 친 부분과 의미가 가장 가까운 것을 고르세요.

**1** The judge is to make a decision today. (can / will / may)

**2** Promises are not to be broken. (must not / will not / cannot)

**3** If you are to succeed, you need to work hard. (want to / decide to / seem to)

**4** Sam and Monica are to be married in November. (will / might / could)

**5** She is to finish the work by seven o'clock. (would / should / might)


## WRITING PRACTICE

우리말과 일치하도록 괄호 안의 말을 바르게 배열하여 문장을 완성하세요.

**1** Nick이 버스에 맨 처음으로 탄 승객이었다. (get, first, the, to, passenger, on)

→ Nick was _____ the bus.

**2** 나는 항공편을 예약하기 위해 여행사에 갔다. (flight, to, a, book)

→ I went to the travel agency _____.

**3** 나는 그 소식을 듣고서 조금 놀랐다. (hear, surprised, to, news, the)

→ I was a little _____.

☑ **CHECK UP** 괄호 안에서 알맞은 것을 고르세요.

**1** It's important (for / of) drivers to be careful. `A-2`

**2** It was polite (for / of) Laura to write to thank us. `A-3`

**3** He is (fast enough / enough fast) to run a mile in four minutes. `B-1`

**4** This plate is (very / so) hot that I can't touch it. `B-2`

**5** They seem (have / to have) a problem with Austin. `B-3`

**A** 빈칸에 for 또는 of를 알맞게 쓰세요. (둘 다 필요하지 않으면 × 표시할 것)

**1** It's helpful _____ students to learn how to swim.

**2** It is dangerous _____ children to play on the roof.

**3** It took _____ me 40 days to break my bad habit.

**4** It was silly _____ me to forget the appointment.

**5** It was nice _____ them to invite us to dinner.

**6** It cost _____ me $30 to take the train to the airport.

**B** 두 문장이 같은 뜻이 되도록 빈칸에 알맞은 말을 쓰세요.

**1** Carol was so fast that she could win the race.

= Carol was _____ _____ _____ _____ the race.

**2** The machine doesn't seem to be working.

= It seems _____ _____ _____ _____ _____ working.

**3** Jim was so lazy that he couldn't finish his homework on time.

= Jim was _____ _____ _____ _____ his homework on time.

**4** The chicken is so spicy that I can't eat it.

= The chicken is _____ _____ _____ _____ _____

_____ .

**C** 괄호 안의 말이 들어갈 위치로 적절한 곳에 ✔ 표시하세요.

**1** It was foolish her to do that again. (of)

**2** The fence is too high me to climb. (for)

**3** They aren't old to see the movie. (enough)

**4** The sign wasn't enough for us to see. (large)

**5** The letter is small that I cannot read it. (so)

**D** 밑줄 친 부분 중 어법상 옳은 것에 ○ 표시하고, 옳지 않은 것은 바르게 고쳐 쓰세요.

**1** You are <u>not enough old</u> to drive. _____

**2** It was <u>very sweet for him</u> to give us a gift. _____

**3** We need ten chairs <u>everyone to have a seat</u>. _____

**4** It was careless <u>of you to say</u> that. _____

**5** I had <u>tomatoes enough to make</u> sauce. _____

---

**WRITING PRACTICE**

우리말과 일치하도록 괄호 안의 말을 알맞은 형태로 바꾸어 문장을 완성하세요.

**1** 수영할 수 있을 만큼 날이 충분히 따뜻하다. (warm, enough)

It is _____ _____ _____ _____.

**2** 그 바지는 내가 입기에는 너무 크다. (big, wear)

The pants are _____ _____ _____ _____ _____ _____.

**3** 그녀가 그를 구출한 것은 용감한 일이었다. (brave, rescue)

It was _____ _____ _____ _____ _____ _____.

**4** 네가 모든 일에 화를 내는 것은 바보 같은 짓이다. (stupid, get)

It's _____ _____ _____ _____ _____ angry at everything.

☑ **CHECK UP** 괄호 안에서 알맞은 것을 고르세요.

**1** Mom told me (clean / to clean) the bathroom.    `A`

**2** I saw him (entering / to enter) the theater.    `B-1`

**3** Let me (drive / to drive) you home.    `B-2`

**4** She had me (do / to do) everything for her.    `B-2`

**5** She helped him (find / found) a new apartment.    `B-2`

**A** 그림과 일치하도록 괄호 안의 말을 이용하여 문장을 완성하세요. (과거시제로 쓸 것)

**1** Mike _____ (see) her _____ _____ (fall down) the stairs.

**2** I _____ (hear) the doorbell _____ (ring) at midnight.

**3** We _____ (watch) the helicopter _____ _____ (take off).

**B** 문장의 밑줄 친 부분을 바르게 고쳐 쓰세요.

**1** Will you <u>help me finding</u> my wallet? _____

**2** He <u>heard the bomb to explode</u>. _____

**3** She <u>had her son to bring</u> a cart. _____

**4** <u>Let me introducing</u> myself. _____

**5** I <u>got Benny took</u> a picture with me. _____

**6** Rainy days <u>make me to feel</u> depressed. _____

**C** 괄호 안에서 어법상 적절하지 <u>않은</u> 하나를 고르세요.

**1** Chris (got / told / had) us to clean the mess.

**2** I (made / heard / watched) him singing in the rain.

**3** We (had / saw / asked) them paint the wall.

**4** Diana (let / had / got) her sister drive her new car.

**5** I helped him (win / to win / winning) first prize.

**D** [보기]에서 알맞은 동사를 골라 적절한 형태로 바꾸어 문장을 완성하세요.

[보기]  play    agree    leave    shake    eat

**1** She felt her room _____ during the earthquake.

**2** I expected you _____ with me on that point.

**3** Brian wanted us _____ the room.

**4** The teacher let us _____ outside.

**5** My mother got me _____ vegetables.

## WRITING PRACTICE

우리말과 일치하도록 [보기]와 괄호 안의 말을 이용하여 문장을 완성하세요.

[보기]  feel    get    help

**1** Clara는 뭔가가 어깨에 닿는 느낌이 들었다. (touch)

Clara _____ _____ _____ her on the shoulder.

**2** Dennis는 할머니가 여행가방을 위층으로 옮기는 것을 도와 주었다. (carry)

Dennis _____ his grandmother _____ her suitcase upstairs.

**3** 아버지는 내가 머리를 짧게 자르게 하셨다. (cut)

My father _____ _____ _____ _____ my hair short.

# UNIT 38 동명사의 기초

**☑ CHECK UP** 괄호 안에서 알맞은 것을 고르세요.

1 (Played / Playing) badminton with him was fun. `B · 1`

2 Gwen enjoys (to create / creating) things. `B · 2`

3 My favorite activity is (to reading / reading) poetry. `B · 3`

4 I will work late instead of (working / work) on Sunday. `B · 4`

5 I don't like my father (call / calling) me "Sleepy Head." `C`

**A** [보기]에서 알맞은 동사를 하나씩 골라 동명사 형태로 바꾸어 빈칸을 완성하세요.

[보기]   lose   swim   be   drink   drive   make

1 _____ carrot juice is healthy for you.

2 His job is _____ movies.

3 _____ alone makes me feel free.

4 Do you enjoy _____ cars?

5 _____ in the morning is good for _____ weight.

**B** 두 문장이 같은 뜻이 되도록 빈칸에 알맞은 말을 쓰세요.

1 Would you mind if I used your phone for a minute?

= Would you mind _____ _____ your phone for a minute?

2 It's not safe for you to go alone.

= _____ _____ is not safe for you.

3 It is too tiring for my mother to walk so far.

= _____ so far is too tiring for my mother.

4 Learning a foreign language takes a long time.

= _____ takes a long time _____ _____ a foreign language.

**C** 문장의 밑줄 친 부분을 바르게 고쳐 쓰세요.

**1** Doing acrobatics <u>require</u> a lot of energy.　　　　　_____

**2** <u>Fish in rivers</u> is Adam's favorite hobby.　　　　　_____

**3** He loves his car and enjoys <u>to drive</u> it.　　　　　_____

**4** Her hobby is <u>collect stamps</u>.　　　　　_____

**5** Would you mind <u>I eating</u> some of your salad?　　　　　_____


**D** 우리말과 일치하도록 괄호 안의 말을 바르게 배열하여 문장을 완성하세요.

**1** 버스를 타는 것은 편리하다. (bus, is, taking, convenient, the)

→ _____ .

**2** Ian은 매운 음식을 먹는 것을 싫어한다. (spicy, hates, food, eating)

→ Ian _____ .

**3** Donald는 친구들에게 편지 보내는 것을 즐긴다. (to his friends, letters, enjoys, sending)

→ Donald _____ .

**4** 제가 문을 닫아도 될까요? (you, the door, my, mind, shutting, would)

→ _____ ?


## WRITING PRACTICE

괄호 안의 말을 써서 다음 [조건]에 맞는 문장을 완성하세요.

**[조건]**　　주어진 동사를 동명사 형태로 바꿀 것

**1** 그는 아이들에게 영어를 가르치는 것을 자랑스러워 한다. (teach)

He is proud of _____ _____ _____ children.

**2** 돈을 저축하는 것은 여러 가지 이유로 중요하다. (save)

_____ _____ _____ _____ for many reasons.

**3** A: 저를 위해 이 편지를 번역해주시면 안 될까요? (translate)　　B: 그럼요, 해 드릴게요.

A: Would you mind _____ _____ _____ for me?

B : _____ _____ _____ .

↗ **CHECK UP** 괄호 안에서 알맞은 것을 고르세요.

**1** It has stopped (to rain / raining) and the sun is shining. **A**

**2** Julia wants (to become / becoming) an actress. **B**

**3** Maggie likes (to take / take) a bath before she goes to bed. **C**

**4** Don't forget (to close / closing) the door when you leave. **D-1**

**5** I remember (to go / going) fishing with my father when I was young. **D-1**

**A** 괄호 안의 말을 알맞은 형태로 바꾸어 문장을 완성하세요.

**1** Megan learned _____ (drive) when she was 22.

**2** I avoided _____ (answer) his questions.

**3** Did you finish _____ (write) your report for class?

**4** We decided _____ (spend) our holidays on a Greek island.

**5** We planned _____ (jump) rope at the park every morning.

**6** She gave up _____ (teach) for some reason.

**B** 괄호 안에서 알맞은 것을 고르세요. (둘 다 알맞을 경우 모두 고를 것)

**1** I had a flat tire, so I had to stop (to change / changing) it.

**2** I remember (to see / seeing) the car accident last month.

**3** The teacher began (to read / reading) the textbook.

**4** Can you stop (to talk / talking), please? I'm studying!

**5** He wants to continue (to work / working) for his company.

**6** I'll never forget (to fly / flying) over the valley. It was wonderful.

**7** The bank charged her extra because she forgot (to pay / paying) the bill on time.

**C**  문장의 밑줄 친 부분을 바르게 고쳐 쓰세요.

1  I wish <u>becoming</u> a doctor.  _____

2  He <u>refused accepting</u> my advice.  _____

3  The child <u>learned walking</u> quickly.  _____

4  They are <u>considering to travel</u> to Italy.  _____

5  Mr. Lee <u>quit to smoke</u> because his wife didn't like it.  _____

6  I'd like to <u>avoid to meet</u> him forever.  _____

**D**  괄호 안에서 알맞은 것을 고르세요.

1  They didn't (enjoy / want / finish) to fall asleep so early.

2  I gave him my number and he promised (to call / calling / call) me.

3  All of us (agreed / minded / gave up) to stay there again.

4  She tried (to lose / losing / lost) weight for more than six weeks.

5  The bookstore stopped (to sell / selling / sold) books online.

6  I didn't (decide / hope / mind) waiting.

## WRITING PRACTICE

우리말과 일치하도록 [보기]와 괄호 안의 말을 이용하여 문장을 완성하세요.

[보기]  stop    delay    forget

1  나는 콘택트 렌즈를 끼는 것을 잊었다. (wear)

   I _____ _____ _____ my contact lenses.

2  Rick은 신발 끈을 매려고 걸음을 멈췄다. (tie)

   Rick _____ _____ _____ his shoelaces.

3  Rachel과 Owen은 여름휴가 계획을 세우는 것을 연기했다. (plan)

   Rachel and Owen _____ _____ their summer holiday.

☑ **CHECK UP** 괄호 안에서 알맞은 것을 고르세요.

**1** How (to / about) going downtown? `A`

**2** Robin couldn't help (to agree / agreeing) with Sam. `A`

**3** The documentary is (worth / worthy) watching. `A`

**4** I'm used to (do / doing) the dishes after meals. `B`

**5** She used to (work / working) for the magazine company. `B`

**A** 괄호 안의 말을 알맞은 형태로 바꾸어 빈칸을 완성하세요.

**1** I feel like _____ (go) on a picnic right now.

**2** They were opposed to _____ (pay) such high taxes.

**3** I spent a lot of time _____ (study) for the midterm exam.

**4** The play is worth _____ (see) at a theater.

**5** Helen is busy _____ (plan) for the music festival.

**6** We are looking forward to _____ (work) with you.

**B** 어법상 틀린 부분을 고쳐 문장을 다시 쓰세요.

**1** Kate has trouble to make decisions.

→ _____

**2** Connie used to working at a bank.

→ _____

**3** Frank was used to drive at night.

→ _____

**4** I object to smoke in public places.

→ _____

**5** It's no use to say that we are doing our best.

→ _____

**C** 두 문장이 같은 뜻이 되도록 빈칸에 알맞은 말을 쓰세요.

**1** I couldn't help thinking he was a fool.

= I couldn't _____ _____ _____ he was a fool.

**2** As soon as I got up, I took a shower.

= _____ _____ _____, I took a shower.

**3** What do you say to dancing with me?

= How _____ _____ with me?


**D** 괄호 안에서 알맞은 것을 고르세요.

**1** We (are used to / used to / used) staying up late.

**2** We're looking forward (at / for / to) eating out this weekend.

**3** There is (no / not / no use) taking pictures in the museum.

**4** The guard prevented us (from / for / with) entering the office.

**5** I am (object / opposed / worth) to keeping animals in the house.


## WRITING PRACTICE

우리말과 일치하도록 각 상자 속 어구를 하나씩 연결하여 문장을 완성하세요.

| Charlie | prevented him from | being scolded |
|---|---|---|
| His knee injury | is used to | finding Roy's house |
| We | had trouble | playing in today's game |

**1** 우리는 Roy의 집을 찾는 데 어려움을 겪었다.

→ _____.

**2** 그는 무릎 부상 때문에 오늘 경기에 출전하지 못했다.

→ _____.

**3** Charlie는 꾸중을 듣는 데 익숙하다.

→ _____.

UNIT **41** 분사의 개념 및 역할

정답 및 해설 p.61

⤢ **CHECK UP**

괄호 안에서 알맞은 것을 고르세요.

**1** I found my (stealing / stolen) bike in the park. <kbd>A</kbd>

**2** The hairdresser is (drying / dried) Mary's hair. <kbd>B-1</kbd>

**3** The Bible is (read / readed) all over the world. <kbd>B-1</kbd>

**4** The man (siting / sitting) on a bench is Mr. Brown. <kbd>B-2</kbd>

**5** Don't touch that (boiling water / water boiling). <kbd>B-2</kbd>

**A** 그림과 일치하도록 괄호 안의 말을 알맞은 분사 형태로 바꾸어 문장을 완성하세요.

**1**

The dog is _____ (chase) the cat.

**2**

The lady _____ (sell) fruit is friendly.

**3**

The baby _____ (lie) in the cradle is my niece.

**4**

Jim's _____ (use) car has many problems.

**B** 각 동사의 현재분사형 또는 과거분사형을 빈칸에 쓰세요.

| 동사원형 | 현재분사 | 과거분사 | 동사원형 | 현재분사 | 과거분사 |
|---|---|---|---|---|---|
| **1** go | going | _____ | **2** run | running | _____ |
| **3** drive | _____ | driven | **4** cut | _____ | cut |
| **5** fly | flying | _____ | **6** lay | laying | _____ |

**C** 밑줄 친 부분이 현재분사인지 동명사인지 구분하여 같은 것끼리 그 번호를 쓰세요.

**1** The little puppy jumping around the garden is cute.

**2** The students finished drawing self-portraits.

**3** Sarah loved the idea of making a film together.

**4** All of them are talking on the phone.

**5** Washing machines are usually very heavy.

**6** We had exciting plans for the weekend.

• 현재분사: _____     • 동명사: _____

## WRITING PRACTICE

우리말과 일치하도록 괄호 안의 말을 바르게 배열하여 문장을 완성하세요.

**1** 나는 스위스에서 만들어진 시계를 주문했다. (made, a watch, I, in Switzerland, ordered)

→ _____ .

**2** 나는 수면제를 먹었지만 잠드는 데 아무 도움도 되지 않았다. (took, I, pills, sleeping)

→ _____ , but they didn't help me sleep at all.

**3** 우리에게 빌려 준 모든 돈은 이미 쓰였다. (was, lent, spent, to us)

→ All the money _____ already.

**4** 지난주에 산 그 사과들은 썩었다. (were, the apples, last week, bought, rotten)

→ _____ .

# UNIT 42 현재분사 vs. 과거분사

정답 및 해설 p.62

↗ **CHECK UP** 괄호 안에서 알맞은 것을 고르세요.

**1** I have some (exciting / excited) news for you.  `B-1`

**2** The trip to Michigan was so (tiring / tired).  `B-1`

**3** Emily was (pleasing / pleased) to hear the news.  `B-2`

**4** I feel (depressing / depressed) on rainy days.  `B-2`

**5** Will you have your photo (taken / taking)?  `C-2`

**A** 그림과 일치하도록 주어진 말을 알맞은 분사 형태로 바꾸어 빈칸을 완성하세요.

**1** interest

**2** bore

**3** thrill

Ms. Taylor's French lessons are very _____ .
I am _____ in learning French.

It was such a _____ movie.
We were really _____ .

The roller coaster was _____ .
We were _____ .

**B** 괄호 안의 동사를 알맞은 분사 형태로 바꾸어 빈칸을 완성하세요.

**1** I saw him _____ (startle) by the thunder.

**2** He spent a _____ (relax) evening at home.

**3** I received a letter _____ (write) in English.

**4** There are some people _____ (wait) for the bus.

**5** Aaron had his shirt and pants _____ (wash).

**6** We saw two strangers _____ (enter) the empty house.

**7** It was _____ (fascinate) to watch the ice skaters.

**102** G-ZONE WORKBOOK

**C** 괄호 안에서 알맞은 것을 고르세요.

**1** His life story is so (touching / touched).

**2** She was (amazing / amazed) by the circus performance.

**3** It was (disappointing / disappointed) that they lost the game.

**4** The reporter got totally (confusing / confused).

**5** The girl asked her teacher a lot of (embarrassing / embarrassed) questions.


**D** 자연스러운 대화가 되도록 문장의 밑줄 친 부분을 바르게 고쳐 쓰세요.

**1** A : Cindy was <u>surprise</u> by her aunt's visit. _____

   B : Yes, it was <u>surprise</u> that she came. _____

**2** A : The children were <u>amuse</u> at the amusement park. _____

   B : It was quite an <u>amuse</u> day for them. _____

**3** A : It's so <u>annoy</u> to have to wait in line. _____

   B : I agree. I'm <u>annoy</u>, too. _____


**WRITING PRACTICE**

괄호 안의 말을 써서 다음 [조건]에 맞는 문장을 완성하세요.

[조건]   괄호 안의 동사를 현재분사 또는 과거분사로 바꿀 것

**1** 그 가수의 죽음은 그의 팬들 모두에게 충격적이었다. (shock)

The singer's death _____ _____ to all of his fans.

**2** 당신의 시는 감동적이고 아름답다. (move)

Your poem is _____ _____ _____.

**3** 나는 문이 스스로 닫히는 것을 보았다. (close)

I _____ _____ _____ _____ by itself.

☑ **CHECK UP** **괄호 안에서 알맞은 것을 고르세요.**

**1** (Picking / She picking) up the phone, she dialed a number. `A-2`

**2** (Knowing not / Not knowing) his phone number, I couldn't call him. `A-2`

**3** (Feeling / Felt) cold, Alice turned on the heater. `B-3`

**4** (Speaking generally / Generally speaking), cats are quieter than dogs. `B-4`

**5** She was sitting on a chair with her legs (crossing / crossed). `C`

**A** **문장의 밑줄 친 부분을 분사구문으로 바꾸어 쓰세요.**

**1** <u>When he turned to the right</u>, he could see the station.

→ _____, he could see the station.

**2** <u>As I read the book</u>, I became aware of a problem.

→ _____, I became aware of a problem.

**3** <u>Because Jack was exhausted</u>, he asked his wife to drive.

→ _____, Jack asked his wife to drive.

**4** <u>Because I stayed home all day</u>, I got bored.

→ _____, I got bored.

**B** **[보기]에서 알맞은 말을 하나씩 골라 빈칸을 채우세요.**

[보기]     Generally speaking      Strictly speaking

            Considering that         Judging from

**1** _____ he is 60 years old, he looks very young.

**2** _____, cars should stop at a yellow light.

**3** _____ his voice, he feels bad today.

**4** _____, there are many jobs in the medical field.

**C** 두 문장이 같은 뜻이 되도록 [보기]에서 알맞은 접속사를 하나씩 골라 빈칸을 채우세요.

[보기]   if   because   when

**1** Being hungry, he was not in a good mood.

= _____ he was hungry, he was not in a good mood.

**2** Seeing the beautiful painting, you will never forget it.

= _____ you see the beautiful painting, you will never forget it.

**3** Thinking of my hometown, I feel comfortable.

= _____ I think of my hometown, I feel comfortable.


**D** 우리말과 일치하도록 괄호 안의 말을 바르게 배열하여 문장을 완성하세요.

**1** 아파서, 나는 종일 침대에 있었다. (stayed, I, being, sick, in bed)

→ _____, _____ all day.

**2** 무엇을 해야 할지 몰라서, 그녀는 그저 웃었다. (what to do, not, just, she, knowing, smiled)

→ _____, _____.

**3** 그는 음악을 틀어 놓은 채 잠을 자고 있었다. (with, sleeping, he, playing, was, the music)

→ _____.


## WRITING PRACTICE

우리말과 일치하도록 괄호 안의 말을 알맞은 형태로 바꾸어 문장을 완성하세요.

**1** 주호는 농구를 하다가 다리를 다쳤다. (play, basketball)

→ Juho hurt his leg _____ _____.

**2** 창문을 열고서, 나는 시원한 산들바람을 느꼈다. (open)

→ _____ _____ _____, I felt the cool breeze.

**3** 게임 하는 것이 지겨워져서, 우리는 자전거를 타러 나갔다. (tire, go out)

→ _____ of playing games, we _____ _____ to ride our bikes.

# 실전 TEST 04 Unit 34-43

**1** 다음 중 밑줄 친 동사의 형태가 적절하지 <u>않은</u> 것을 고르세요.

① I don't want <u>to go</u> there by myself.
② I look forward <u>to see</u> you.
③ Is there anything <u>to drink</u>?
④ She woke up <u>to find</u> she was alone.
⑤ We ran in order <u>not to be</u> late.

서술형

**2** 다음 두 문장이 같은 뜻이 되도록 빈칸을 완성하세요.

> She didn't know how to answer the question.

= She didn't know how _____
_____ _____ the question.

**3** 다음 중 [보기]의 밑줄 친 부분과 쓰임이 같은 것을 고르세요.

[보기]  I'm pleased <u>to see</u> you again.

① Tell me what <u>to do</u>.
② I'm sorry <u>to hear</u> that.
③ Would you like <u>to order</u>?
④ If you want <u>to ask</u> a question, feel free to call me.
⑤ You can find plenty of books <u>to read</u> here.

서술형

**[4-5]** 다음 우리말과 일치하도록 빈칸에 알맞은 말을 쓰세요.

**4**
> 나를 도와주다니 넌 정말 친절하구나.

→ It's so _____ _____
_____ to help me.

**5**
> 나는 해야 할 숙제가 많다.

→ I have lots of _____ _____
_____.

**6** 다음 중 짝지어진 두 문장의 뜻이 서로 <u>다른</u> 하나를 고르세요.

① My sister is smart enough to solve any problem.
   - My sister is so smart that she can solve any problem.
② Barbara is looking for a part-time job in order to make some money.
   - Barbara is looking for a part-time job so as to make some money.
③ Terry and I were too busy to answer the door.
   - Terry and I were so busy that we could answer the door.
④ It is necessary for Alan to come to class.
   - Alan needs to come to class.
⑤ He was very stupid to say that.
   - It was very stupid of him to say that.

**7** 다음 우리말과 일치하도록 빈칸에 들어갈 말이 바르게 짝 지어진 것을 고르세요.

> • 그는 가슴이 빠르게 뛰는 상태로 그 노래를 들었다.
> He listened to the song with his heart
> _____ quickly.
> • 그녀에게 문제가 있는 것 같다.
> She seems _____ a problem.
> • 무엇이 일어날지 알 수 없다.
> There is no _____ what will
> happen.

① beaten – having – to know
② beaten – to have – to know
③ beating – to have – to know
④ beating – having – knowing
⑤ beating – to have – knowing

**8** 다음 밑줄 친 부분 중 어법상 옳은 것을 고르세요.

> Today ① I'm here to thank Prof. Kim.
> He has helped me a lot. ② To honest,
> I spent most of my first year in college
> having fun with my friends. Now, I know
> it was really ③ foolish for me to waste
> time like that. I had enough ④ time trying
> many things, but I simply didn't think
> about my life. But then Prof. Kim made
> me think about my life and helped ⑤ me
> finding out what I really wanted to do.

①     ②     ③     ④     ⑤

**[9~11]** 다음 밑줄 친 부분 중 어법상 옳지 <u>않은</u> 것을 고르세요.

**9** ① I helped Mom <u>wash</u> the dishes.
② Tim couldn't help <u>get</u> upset.
③ Did you hear someone <u>running</u>?
④ Liz heard a bee <u>buzzing</u> around.
⑤ I need to have my hair <u>cut</u>.

**10** ① Do you mind <u>opening</u> the window?
② The old man stopped <u>to light</u> his cigarette.
③ Oh, I almost forgot <u>calling</u> him! I'll do it right now.
④ We enjoyed <u>skiing</u> very much.
⑤ I remembered <u>to buy</u> milk at the supermarket.

**11** ① I can't understand what you mean. I'm <u>confused</u>.
② I heard <u>depressing</u> news. I'm going to lose my job.
③ It was a <u>tiring</u> job. I need to take a long rest now.
④ I think your behavior at the party was <u>disappointed</u>.
⑤ I was <u>shocked</u> by the news. I didn't expect it at all.

**12** 다음 중 분사구문이 어법상 옳지 <u>않은</u> 것을 고르세요.

① I being depressed, I ate pieces of chocolate.
② Walking along the street, I met an old friend.
③ Living in America, he speaks English well.
④ Turning to the right, you will see the store.
⑤ Not knowing his number, I can't call him.

서술형

**13** 다음 우리말과 일치하도록 괄호 안의 동사를 알맞은 분사 형태로 바꿔 쓰세요.

> 그의 수업은 매우 지루하다. 그래서 나는 그의 수업 시간에 지루해 죽겠다.

→ His lessons are very _____ (bore). So I feel _____ (bore) to death in his class.

**14** 다음 밑줄 친 부분을 괄호 안의 말로 바꿔도 의미가 비슷한 것을 모두 고르세요. (2개)

① Do you mind <u>closing the window</u>? (if I close the window)
② The pianist began <u>to play</u> her biggest hit. (playing)
③ Remember <u>to tell</u> me before you leave. (telling)
④ They <u>seem to be</u> at home. (It seems that they are)
⑤ We <u>are used to skipping</u> lunch. (used to skip)

**15** 다음 밑줄 친 부분 중 어법상 옳은 것을 고르세요.

① I expect <u>seeing</u> you again soon.
② Let me <u>to introduce</u> myself.
③ What are you planning <u>to do</u> this weekend?
④ Stop <u>to make</u> noise, please!
⑤ I have decided <u>taking</u> the challenge.

**16** 다음 밑줄 친 단어 중 성격이 나머지와 다른 하나를 고르세요.

① He watched the horses <u>running</u> across the farm.
② He stood still <u>listening</u> to the announcement.
③ Don't you smell something <u>burning</u>?
④ We were the only guests <u>staying</u> at the hotel.
⑤ I can't stop <u>thinking</u> about the result of my English exam.

**17** 다음 중 밑줄 친 부분을 가장 적절하게 해석한 것을 고르세요.

① He denied <u>dating Susan</u>.
   (Susan과 사귀고 있다는 것을)
② People try <u>to change</u> themselves, but it's not easy. (시험 삼아 바꿔보다)
③ Leo was <u>used to the old computer</u>. (오래된 컴퓨터를 사용했다)
④ We haven't decided <u>where to go</u>. (어디로 갈지 말지를)
⑤ I can't <u>forget shaking hands</u> with Yoo Jae-suk!
   (악수해야 한다는 것을 잊어버리다)

**18** 다음 중 [보기]의 밑줄 친 분사구문의 용법과 가장 가까운 것을 고르세요.

> [보기]  <u>Singing softly</u>, she entered the house.

① <u>Being sick</u>, he was absent from school.
② <u>Watching the news on TV every morning</u>, I know all the current issues.
③ <u>Smiling brightly</u>, he waved his hands.
④ <u>Having some work to do</u>, I can't go out now.
⑤ <u>Living near her house</u>, he sometimes sees her.

서술형

**19** 다음 괄호 안의 말을 알맞은 형태로 바꾸어 글을 완성하세요.

> Companies use advertising to get consumers ⓐ _____ (buy) their products. Advertisements are everywhere — on television, on the radio, in newspapers, in magazines, and on billboards. Advertising agencies believe that if they show you the same ad enough times, they can make you prefer a certain product. They want you to believe that their product makes clothes cleaner, lasts longer, protects you better, or makes you more attractive.
> Ads are not only for products; they are also for services. An ad may try to tell you where to buy a nice car, where to get good legal advice, or where to have your eyes ⓑ _____ (examine).

서술형

**[20-21]** 다음 우리말과 일치하도록 괄호 안에서 필요한 단어만을 골라 바르게 배열하세요.

**20**
> 그는 첫 기차를 탈 수 있을 만큼 일찍 일어났다.
> (to, too, early, fast, catch, enough)

→ He got up _____ _____

_____ _____ the first train.

**21**
> 그 의사는 그녀의 간호사에게 내 체온을 재라고 했다.
> (to, the doctor, take, her nurse, had, taken)

→ _____ _____ _____

_____ _____ _____

my temperature.

**22** 다음 밑줄 친 부분 중 어법상 옳지 <u>않은</u> 것을 고르세요.

> Before coming to the U.S., people usually have ideas about what they will see when they get there. Some people find that the U.S. is better than they ① <u>expected</u>. Others find that it is worse. Many people say that they are ② <u>surprised</u> to learn that it isn't easy to become rich quickly in the U.S. Others are ③ <u>amazed to see</u> so many poor and homeless people in such a rich country. Some are ④ <u>disappointed</u> to find that health care is so expensive. Other people are ⑤ <u>surprising to find</u> that there is so much crime and that people in some places are afraid to walk on the street at night.

①      ②      ③      ④      ⑤

↗ **CHECK UP** 　**괄호 안에서 알맞은 것을 고르세요.**

**1** I want to be a pilot (who / which) flies helicopter. 　C-1

**2** A barber is a person (who / which) cuts men's hair. 　C-1

**3** It is important to eat food (who / that) is good for you. 　C-2

**4** Look at the bird (who / which) is feeding her babies! 　C-2

**5** The boy (who sleeping / sleeping) in the bed is my younger brother. 　C-3

**A** 　**빈칸에 관계대명사 who 또는 which를 알맞게 쓰세요.**

**1** Do you know the guy _____ is standing by the red car?

**2** One of the customers _____ came tonight forgot his jacket.

**3** Korea is a country _____ has a lot of mountains.

**4** They took a train _____ goes to Seoul station.

**B** 　**그림과 일치하도록 괄호 안의 말과 관계대명사를 이용하여 문장을 완성하세요.**

**1** 　　　　　　　　**2** 　　　　　　　　**3**

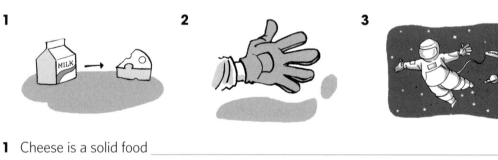

**1** Cheese is a solid food _____.
(be made from milk)

**2** A glove is a piece of clothing _____.
(cover your fingers and hands)

**3** An astronaut is a person _____.
(travel and work in space)

**C**      괄호 안에서 알맞은 것을 고르세요.

**1** You should wear shoes that (match / matches) your dress.

**2** Where is the (woman / shop) which sells ginseng?

**3** We should find the (truck / man) who parked here.

**4** He introduced me to a woman who (was / were) an actress.

**5** My neighbor has a dog (that / who) barks all night long.


**D**      문장의 밑줄 친 부분을 바르게 고쳐 쓰세요.

**1** The person is baking cookies is her elder sister.        _____

**2** Can you suggest a shirt who will make me look thinner?        _____

**3** I like books which is based on true stories.        _____

**4** Monica is a person who she can help you.        _____

**5** The trains that carry cargo doesn't stop at this station.        _____


## WRITING PRACTICE

괄호 안의 말을 써서 다음 [조건]에 맞는 문장을 완성하세요.

**[조건]**    관계대명사 who 또는 which를 이용할 것

**1** 양파는 눈물이 나게 하는 채소이다. (make, cry)

Onions are vegetables _____ _____ you _____ .

**2** 이탈리아 출신인 그 남자는 요리사이다. (come from, be)

The man _____ _____ _____ Italy _____ a cook.

**3** 그는 개와 함께 조깅하고 있는 저 여자를 안다. (know, jog)

He _____ that woman _____ _____ _____ with her dog.

**☑ CHECK UP**  괄호 안에서 알맞은 것을 고르세요.

**1** She is the woman (who / which) Hans wanted to marry.　　`A-1`

**2** The teacher lectured on a subject which I was (interested / interested in).　　`B-1`

**3** The man to (whom / that) I spoke was attractive.　　`B-2`

**4** I know a Korean girl (who / whose) English is almost perfect.　　`C-1`

**5** Can you show me (that / what) you bought?　　`D`

**A**　[보기]에서 알맞은 말을 골라 빈칸을 채우세요.

> [보기]　who　　which　　what　　whose

**1** My friend _____ bag was stolen called the police.

**2** _____ Maria told you was true.

**3** She is the lady _____ I sold my car to.

**4** I have a book _____ Carla wanted to borrow.

**5** This is not _____ Judy wants to have.

**B**　두 문장이 같은 뜻이 되도록 빈칸에 알맞은 말을 쓰세요.

**1** This is the house. The novelist wrote her first novel in the house.

　　= This is the house _____ _____ the novelist wrote her first novel.

**2** This is the mistake. I am responsible for it.

　　= This is the mistake _____ I am responsible _____.

**3** Everyone was surprised at the thing that I showed them.

　　= Everyone was surprised at _____ I showed them.

**4** The man's voice is deep. He is an actor.

　　= The man _____ voice is deep _____ an actor.

**C**   괄호 안에서 알맞은 것을 고르세요.

**1** This is exactly (what / that) I wanted.

**2** Snakes are an animal of (which / that) I'm afraid.

**3** That's the woman (who / whose) dog bit me.

**4** (What / That) surprised me was his reaction to my words.

**5** There are many words (which / whose) meanings I've never learned.

**D**   문장의 밑줄 친 부분을 바르게 고쳐 쓰세요.

**1** It was the party <u>at that</u> I met her.                    _____

**2** She's <u>an artist of</u> I've never heard.                   _____

**3** Here's <u>the room which</u> the kids can play or sleep.      _____

**4** He's the neighbor <u>who son</u> is ill.                      _____

**5** She didn't <u>believe that I said</u> about her son.          _____

**6** <u>The team who he joined</u> won this year's championship.   _____

---

**WRITING PRACTICE**

우리말과 일치하도록 [보기]의 관계대명사와 괄호 안의 동사를 이용하여 문장을 완성하세요.

[보기]   which      what      whose

**1** 나는 내 아버지가 나를 위해 요리한 것을 먹었다. (cook)

I ate _____ _____ _____ _____ for me.

**2** 내가 잠을 잔 침대는 불편했다. (sleep)

The bed on _____ _____ _____ was uncomfortable.

**3** 전주는 음식이 아주 맛있는 도시이다. (be)

Jeonju is a city _____ food _____ very good.

# UNIT 46 관계부사

정답 및 해설 p.70

⌐ CHECK UP  괄호 안에서 알맞은 것을 고르세요.

**1** This is the city (where / when) Steve Jobs was born.  `B-1`

**2** He recommended some places (in where / where) we can have nice seafood.  `B-1`

**3** I can't forget the day (where / when) we first came to this town.  `B-2`

**4** Is there any reason (when / why) I should be here?  `B-3`

**5** Look at (the way / the way how) Karen is dressed!  `B-4`

## A
[보기]에서 알맞은 말을 하나씩 골라 빈칸을 채우세요.

[보기]  where    why    how    when

**1** I asked them _____ I could get to the nearest theater.

**2** I remember the moment _____ we first met.

**3** Isn't this the place _____ you got married?

**4** I tried to explain the reason _____ I couldn't do my homework.

## B
밑줄 친 부분 중 어법상 옳은 것에 ○ 표시하고, 옳지 않은 것은 바르게 고쳐 쓰세요.

**1** I don't know <u>the way how</u> he moved that heavy rock.  _____

**2** Do you remember <u>the café when</u> we met last month?  _____

**3** The apartment <u>on which he lives</u> is very modern.  _____

**4** Do you know the reason <u>why she said</u> that?  _____

**5** She forgot <u>where the place</u> she parked.  _____

**6** Can you tell me <u>the reason where</u> you left him?  _____

**7** This is <u>the day how</u> Korea got its first medal.  _____

**C** 알맞은 것끼리 짝지어 문장을 완성하세요.

**1** I'd like to know the way   •      • (a) when the weather is usually the coldest.

**2** Please tell me the reason   •      • (b) she solved the problem.

**3** The library is the place   •      • (c) where I spend most of my time.

**4** January is the month   •      • (d) why she's not here.

**D** 두 문장이 같은 뜻이 되도록 [보기]에서 알맞은 말을 하나씩 골라 빈칸을 채우세요.

[보기]    for which      the way      in which      on which

**1** March 19, 2010, was the day when my grandfather passed away.

= March 19, 2010, was the day _____ _____ my grandfather passed away.

**2** I like how you styled your hair.

= I like _____ _____ you styled your hair.

**3** I went to the place where the photo had been taken.

= I went to the place _____ _____ the photo had been taken.

**4** Did she tell you the reason why she didn't come?

= Did she tell you the reason _____ _____ she didn't come?

---

## WRITING PRACTICE

우리말과 일치하도록 괄호 안의 말을 바르게 배열하여 문장을 완성하세요.

**1** 2016년은 내가 중학교에 입학한 해이다. (when, entered, the year, I, middle school)

→ 2016 was _____.

**2** 네가 그것을 어떻게 보느냐에 달려 있다. (how, look at it, you, depends on)

→ It _____.

**3** 너는 Randy가 열쇠를 숨기는 장소를 아니? (where, hides, the place, his key, Randy)

→ Do you know _____?

**CHECK UP**    괄호 안에서 알맞은 것을 고르세요.

**1** I had lunch with my friend, (that / who) told me a funny story.    `A-1`

**2** I called Sana at nine, (why / when) she was eating breakfast.    `A-2`

**3** I'll buy you (whatever / however) you want.    `B`

**4** I'll be impressed by (whoever / wherever) can solve this problem.    `B`

**5** (Whenever / Whatever) spring comes, I feel refreshed.    `C`

---

**A**    밑줄 친 관계사가 가리키는 것을 문장에서 찾아 영어로 쓰세요.

**1** I have a dog, <u>which</u> I keep in my yard.    _____

**2** Please visit me at noon, <u>when</u> I won't be so busy.    _____

**3** I went to Florence in 2010, <u>where</u> I met my husband.    _____

**4** Henry didn't say anything, <u>which</u> made me upset.    _____

**5** Eunbi met a photographer, <u>who</u> works for a magazine.    _____

**6** The subway was delayed, <u>which</u> caused us to be late.    _____

**7** It'll snow tomorrow, <u>which</u> is unusual.    _____

---

**B**    [보기]에서 알맞은 말을 하나씩 골라 빈칸을 채우세요.

[보기]    who    which    that    when    where

**1** John has two sons, _____ respect their father.

**2** They went to Jeju Island, _____ they stayed for a month.

**3** Sunny visited her grandmother _____ lives in the country.

**4** She traveled alone in the summer, _____ it was hot and sunny.

**5** I have a blue sweater, _____ my mother made for me when I was young.

**C** 두 문장이 같은 뜻이 되도록 [보기]의 말과 알맞은 관계대명사를 이용하여 빈칸을 채우세요.

[보기]    anyone        anything        no matter

**1** Whoever wants the map can have it.

= _____ _____ wants the map can have it.

**2** You can wear whatever you like.

= You can wear _____ _____ you like.

**3** Whichever you choose, I hope you'll enjoy it.

= _____ _____ _____ you choose, I hope you'll enjoy it.

**4** Whatever you do, do it as well as you can.

= _____ _____ _____ you do, do it as well as you can.


**D** 괄호 안에서 알맞은 것을 고르세요.

**1** Please take a seat (wherever / however) you like.

**2** (However / Whatever) late you may be, be sure to call me.

**3** I want to eat (whenever / wherever) there is an air conditioner.

**4** You may come to my house (whenever / wherever) you want.

**5** No matter (how / when) young you are, you should take care of your health.


**WRITING PRACTICE**

우리말과 일치하도록 적절한 관계사와 괄호 안의 동사를 이용하여 문장을 완성하세요.

**1** 내가 어디에 있든지, 나는 너를 절대 잊지 않을 것이다. (be)

_____ _____ _____, I will never forget you.

**2** 무슨 일이 일어나도, 그녀는 항상 나의 가장 친한 친구일 것이다. (happen)

No _____ _____ _____, she'll always be my best friend.

**3** 내가 주방에 들어갔는데, 그곳에 아침 식사가 준비되어 있었다. (be prepared)

I went into the kitchen, _____ breakfast _____ _____.

# 접속사의 기본 개념,
# 등위접속사(and, but, or, so)

정답 및 해설 p.73

↗ **CHECK UP**    괄호 안에서 알맞은 것을 고르세요.

**1** Doctors (and / but) nurses work in hospitals.    B·1

**2** Hurry up, (and / or) we'll be late.    B·2

**3** Eat more vegetables, (and / or) you'll lose weight.    B·2

**4** Neither Minho's father (or / nor) his mother speaks English.    C

**5** (Both / Not only) oranges and apples are good for your health.    C

**A**    [보기]에서 알맞은 말을 하나씩 골라 빈칸을 채우세요.

[보기]    but    so    and    or

**1** Thailand is beautiful, _____ the people are friendly.

**2** Looks are important, _____ they're not everything.

**3** I was hungry, _____ I ate a piece of bread and an apple.

**4** We can go to the park _____ the river to have a picnic.

**B**    두 문장이 같은 뜻이 되도록 빈칸에 알맞은 말을 써서 문장을 완성하세요.

**1** If you lose that key, you'll have to pay for it.

= Don't _____ .

**2** Run, and you'll catch the bus in time.

= If you _____ .

**3** Tania was wise as well as beautiful.

= Tania was not only _____ .

**4** I don't know or care about the problem.

= I neither _____ .

**C**    알맞은 것끼리 짝지어 문장을 완성하세요.

1 Jeremy took a taxi,          •          • (a) or disagree with the idea.

2 Let me know if you agree   •          • (b) nor I went to the festival.

3 Neither my friend          •          • (c) so we went to the library.

4 We had to study for the test, •       • (d) but he was still late for school.


**D**    우리말과 일치하도록 괄호 안의 말을 바르게 배열하여 문장을 완성하세요.

1 Max는 간호사가 아니라 의사이다. (a doctor, not, but, a nurse)

   → Max is _____.

2 내 아버지는 나의 멘토이자 가장 친한 친구이다. (but also, my mentor, not only, my best friend)

   → My father is _____.

3 나는 칠레 또는 아르헨티나에 가고 싶다. (go to, or, either, Argentina, Chile)

   → I want to _____.

4 Zoe는 맑은 날과 눈 오는 날 둘 다 좋아한다. (snowy, sunny, days, and, both)

   → Zoe likes _____.

5 그녀는 토마토, 양배추 그리고 셀러리를 샀다. (tomatoes, celery, cabbage, and)

   → She bought _____.


## WRITING PRACTICE

우리말과 일치하도록 [보기]의 접속사와 괄호 안의 말을 이용하여 문장을 완성하세요.

[보기]    as well as      or       but

1 정말 미안해. 하지만 그건 내 잘못이 아니었어. (fault)

   I'm terribly sorry, _____.

2 네 코트를 입어라. 그렇지 않으면 넌 감기에 걸릴 것이다. (put on)

   _____ you'll catch a cold.

3 셰익스피어는 작가일 뿐만 아니라 배우이기도 했다. (writer, actor)

   Shakespeare was _____.

⊡ **CHECK UP**  **괄호 안에서 알맞은 것을 고르세요.**

**1** Vincent prepared dinner, (that / and) Wendy watched TV.　　　A·3

**2** Debby realized (if / that) she had made a mistake.　　　B·1

**3** I don't know (if / that) it's cold outside or not.　　　B·2

**4** I wonder where (he is / is he) going.　　　C·1

**5** I can't remember if (I closed / did I close) the windows.　　　C·2

**A**　　**밑줄 친 명사절의 역할을 [보기]에서 하나씩 골라 쓰세요.**

[보기]　주어　목적어　동격　보어

**1** The truth is that we all want a better world.　　　_____

**2** It is unbelievable that she got all A's.　　　_____

**3** I wonder if it will rain tomorrow.　　　_____

**4** The fact that Angela was late again made me upset.　　　_____

**B**　　**예시와 같이 주어진 의문문을 빈칸에 간접의문문으로 바꿔 쓰세요.**

**0** Where did you see him?

　→ Please tell me where you saw him.

**1** Did I have that book?

　→ I'm not sure _____.

**2** Is the movie playing?

　→ I wonder _____.

**3** When did she come to see me?

　→ I don't know _____.

**4** What country is Tim from?

　→ I don't remember _____.

**C**     두 문장을 **that** 또는 **if**를 사용하여 한 문장으로 만드세요.

**1** It is true. Hair grows faster at night.

→ It is _____.

**2** I can't remember. Did I take my medicine?

→ I can't remember _____.

**3** I don't know. Did she tell you the story?

→ I don't know _____.


**D**     어법상 <u>틀린</u> 부분을 고쳐 문장을 다시 쓰세요.

**1** I believe. That we will win the race.

→ _____

**2** Do you think what Dave should do?

→ _____

**3** I wonder that she is mad at me or not.

→ _____

**4** Bruno asked me that I could join the team.

→ _____


## WRITING PRACTICE

우리말과 일치하도록 괄호 안의 말을 바르게 배열하여 문장을 완성하세요.

**1** 스트레스가 암을 유발할 수 있다는 것은 사실이다. (a fact, stress, it, is, can cause, that)

→ _____ cancer.

**2** 내가 가스 밸브를 잠갔는지 확실히 모르겠다. (not, turned off, sure, I, whether, I'm)

→ _____ the gas.

**3** 화장실이 어디 있는지 가르쳐 주실래요? (where, can, me, the restroom, tell, is, you)

→ _____ ?

↗ **CHECK UP**    괄호 안에서 알맞은 것을 고르세요.

**1** I haven't seen him (since / after) he went to Peru.    **A**

**2** Sam retired (because / because of) ill health.    **B**

**3** (Though / Because) he was tired, he couldn't sleep.    **C**

**4** I can't help you (if / unless) you tell me your problem.    **C**

**5** Walter was (so / such) weak that he could hardly walk.    **D**

**A**    두 문장이 같은 뜻이 되도록 빈칸에 알맞은 말을 쓰세요.

**1** Eric was in a good mood because the weather was nice.

= Eric was in a good mood _____ _____ the nice weather.

**2** Doris washed his face after she had breakfast.

= Doris had breakfast _____ she washed his face.

**3** If you don't read the news, you won't know what's happening.

= _____ you read the news, you won't know what's happening.

**4** The movie was so good that I watched it 15 times.

= It was _____ _____ good movie that I watched it 15 times.

**B**    [보기]에서 밑줄 친 as와 뜻이 가장 가까운 것을 골라 쓰세요.

[보기]    while     in the same way     since

**1** Leave everything just <u>as</u> it is.    _____

**2** <u>As</u> I ate my ice cream, I watched people walk by.    _____

**3** Shall we stop for coffee, <u>as</u> we have some extra time?    _____

**4** I stayed home, <u>as</u> I was feeling sick.    _____

**5** Jina saw a bluebird <u>as</u> she walked in the park.    _____

**C** 문장의 밑줄 친 부분을 바르게 고쳐 쓰세요.

**1** Unless you aren't busy, let's have dinner together. _____

**2** I like ice cream because of it's cold and sweet. _____

**3** If you pay a fee, you cannot get in the museum. _____

**4** She was such shocked that she didn't know what to say. _____

**5** She is so strong what she can lift her brother. _____

**6** Stand up too that you can see better. _____


**D** 괄호 안에서 어법상 적절하지 않은 하나를 고르세요.

**1** We went jogging (until / as soon as / as long as) the sun set.

**2** (Although / Because / Though) Marco had a car, he had never driven it.

**3** I usually brush my teeth (before / after / until) I eat breakfast.

**4** (As / Since / Because of) the sign was written in Japanese, I couldn't read it.

**5** I was thinking about you (when / while / as soon as) I walked alone.


## WRITING PRACTICE

우리말과 일치하도록 괄호 안의 말을 이용하여 문장을 완성하세요.

**1** 네가 갑자기 움직이지 않는다면, 그 개는 너를 물지 않을 거야. (bite)

_____ you move suddenly, the dog _____ _____ you.

**2** 그는 말을 너무 빨리 해서 나는 그의 말을 잘 알아들을 수가 없었다. (fast)

He spoke _____ _____ _____ I _____ quite understand his words.

**3** 네가 너무 빠르게 운전하지 않겠다고 약속하는 한, 내 차를 빌릴 수 있다. (promise)

_____ _____ _____ you _____ not to drive too fast, you can borrow

my car.

**1** 다음 우리말에 해당하는 적절한 접속사를 고르세요.

> I don't care about his personality
> <u>~하는 한</u> he works hard for me.

① even though    ② unless

③ as long as    ④ though

⑤ so that

**[2-4]** 다음 빈칸에 들어갈 알맞은 말을 고르세요.

**2** She did very well in the contest, _____ pleased her parents.

① that    ② what    ③ when

④ which    ⑤ where

**3** _____ plays the game can win a prize.

① Who    ② Whom    ③ That

④ Whoever    ⑤ Whatever

**4** Take _____ book you want from the box.

① whichever ② whoever ③ it

④ how    ⑤ why

**5** 다음 빈칸에 공통으로 들어갈 알맞은 말을 고르세요.

> • Please check _____ there are any mistakes in my paper.
> • Let's discuss _____ or not we can continue to invest in this business.

① if    ② that    ③ when

④ what    ⑤ whether

서술형

**[6-8]** 다음 두 문장이 같은 뜻이 되도록 빈칸을 완성하세요.

**6**

> He asked me "When will she visit me?"

= He asked me when _____ would _____ him.

**7**

> I found a book. Its cover was black.

= I found a book _____ cover was black.

**8**

> This is the house. My family lived there for three years.

= This is the house _____ my family lived for three years.

**9** 다음 괄호 안에서 알맞은 것을 고르세요.

(1) History is the subject in (whom / which / that) I'm most interested.

(2) The boy (whom / which / what) I believed to be honest deceived me.

(3) It is a French word (whose / which / what) I know.

**[10-11] 다음 밑줄 친 부분 중 어법상 옳지 않은 것을 고르세요.**

**10** ① Either butter <u>or</u> cheese is fine.
② Both Susan <u>and</u> Patrick are interested in classical music.
③ He came not to help but <u>to hinder</u> us.
④ Neither Sam <u>or</u> his parents were at home.
⑤ Not only you <u>but also</u> he is in the wrong.

**11** ① I don't know <u>when the concert starts</u>.
② <u>Do you think how old he is?</u>
③ I'm not sure <u>if she had lunch</u>.
④ She asked <u>if I wanted to sing</u>.
⑤ I wonder <u>if he is Japanese or not</u>.

**12** 다음 중 [보기]의 밑줄 친 부분과 같은 용법으로 쓰인 것을 고르세요.

[보기] This is <u>what</u> I want.

① <u>What</u> a nice guy he is!
② I don't know <u>what</u> to do.
③ <u>What</u> do you want to be in the future?
④ Do you know <u>what</u> time he left the office?
⑤ <u>What</u> I need is a glass of water.

서술형
**13** 다음 글을 읽고, 우리말과 일치하도록 문장을 완성하세요.

Scientists discovered *fossils of a new *dinosaur in India. At first, (1) (그들은 그 공룡이 식물을 먹었는지 아니면 고기를 먹었는지 알지 못했다.) Luckily, a farmer found a fossil of its skull in his field. It had large teeth for tearing meat. Therefore, (2) (그 공룡은 고기를 먹은 것이 확실했다.)

*fossil 화석  *dinosaur 공룡

(1) they didn't know _____ the dinosaur ate plants or meat.

(2) _____ was certain _____ the dinosaur ate meat.

**14** 다음 우리말을 영어로 바르게 옮기지 <u>않은</u> 것을 고르세요.

① 지금 출발해라. 그렇지 않으면 회사에 지각할 것이다.

→ Leave now, or you will be late for work.

② 꼭대기가 눈으로 덮여 있는 저 산을 보아라.

→ Look at the mountain whose top is covered with snow.

③ 네가 원하는 한, 너는 우리와 함께 머물러도 된다.

→ You can stay with us as long as you like.

④ 나는 우리가 스키 타러 갈 만한 좋은 장소를 안다.

→ I know a good place which we can go skiing.

⑤ 비록 그는 오래전에 죽었지만, 그들은 그를 잊지 않았다.

→ Even though he died a long time ago, they haven't forgotten him.

**15** 다음 중 어법상 옳지 <u>않은</u> 것을 고르세요.

① Can you tell me the way how this machine works?

② He couldn't understand the reason why he got fired.

③ This is the lake where I used to swim when I was young.

④ Does anybody know the time when she will be back?

⑤ The store from which I bought strawberry cakes closed.

**[16–17]** 다음 글을 읽고, 물음에 답하세요.

> The Wright brothers are the people (1) _____ I admire most. <u>My friends often ask me, "Why do you like them so much?"</u> The reason is that they were both *ingenious. They made the first airplane flight in 1903. The airplane (2) _____ they invented only flew for 12 seconds. After that, they designed many other airplanes. I've studied all the airplanes they designed.
>
> *ingenious 독창적인

**16** 빈칸 (1), (2)에 알맞은 관계대명사를 쓰세요.

**17** 밑줄 친 문장을 간접의문문으로 만들 때, 빈칸에 알맞은 단어를 쓰세요.

> → My friends often ask me _____ I _____ _____ so much.

**18** 다음 중 어법상 옳은 것을 고르세요.

① Give me the book who is on the desk.

② She needs a pencil which she can write.

③ I know a girl whose father is a pilot.

④ I know the man dance on the street.

⑤ That is the man for I was looking.

**19** 다음 중 짝지어진 두 문장의 뜻이 서로 <u>다른</u> 것을 고르세요.

① He speaks Chinese as well as Spanish.
- He speaks not only Spanish but also Chinese.

② Drink at least eight glasses of water, and you'll be healthy.
- If you drink at least eight glasses of water, you'll be healthy.

③ The hotel located on Main Street is the best one in town.
- The hotel that is located on Main Street is the best one in town.

④ She is so strong that she can cope with a lot of stress.
- She isn't strong enough to cope with a lot of stress.

⑤ I liked the scene where she found out the truth.
- I liked the scene in which she found out the truth.

**20** 다음 중 빈칸에 들어갈 말이 바르게 짝지어진 것을 고르세요.

> • _____ I heard the news, I called Michael.
> • Call me before you _____.
> • You should wait _____ I call.

① If – leave – since
② If – will leave – till
③ When – leave – since
④ As soon as – leave – till
⑤ As soon as – will leave – till

**[21-23]** 다음 글을 읽고, 물음에 답하세요.

> Aunt Nancy is the woman working with my mom. I call her "aunt" because she cares about me. <u>For my birthday ⓐ every year, she gives me ⓑ a sweater ⓒ she has made ⓓ herself ⓔ.</u> I love her cat whose name is Joy. What Joy likes best _____ (be) a can of cat food. I always bring her a can.

**21** 위 글에서 'who is'가 들어갈 수 있는 부분을 찾아 ✔ 표시 하세요.

**22** 밑줄 친 문장에서 관계대명사가 생략된 부분을 고르고, 들어갈 수 있는 관계대명사를 쓰세요.

**23** 괄호 안의 동사를 알맞은 형태로 바꾸어 빈칸을 완성하세요. (현재시제로 쓸 것)

**24** 다음 중 어법상 <u>틀린</u> 곳을 찾아 바르게 고쳐 쓰세요.

> There are many things that make your life easier. Wherever you go, you can check your email on the phone. Whenever you want, you can find a lot of information on the Internet. These are who we call modern conveniences.

_____ → _____

↗ **CHECK UP**　　괄호 안에서 알맞은 것을 고르세요.

**1** If she (is / were) not sick, she could go hiking with us. 　　A

**2** If I had a million dollars, I (will / would) donate half to charity. 　　A

**3** If we (knew / had known) how to ski, we could have more fun in winter. 　　A

**4** If I (have heard / had heard) the phone ring, I'd have answered it. 　　B

**5** If she hadn't driven so fast, she'd (pass / have passed) the driving test. 　　B

**A**　　괄호 안의 동사를 알맞은 형태로 바꾸어 빈칸을 완성하세요.

**1** If it _____ (rain) tomorrow, we'll visit a museum.

**2** If you _____ (mix) oil and water, the oil stays on top of the water.

**3** If aliens _____ (come) to Earth, what would you do?

**4** If you _____ (pay) more attention, you wouldn't have burned the rice.

**5** If I _____ (wear) my helmet, I wouldn't have been seriously injured.

**B**　　괄호 안의 말을 알맞은 형태로 바꾸어 문장을 완성하세요.

**1** We _____ (can get) there in an hour if we _____
(have) a car, but we don't have one.

**2** You _____ (will do) better in school if you _____
(spend) more time studying, but you never open a book outside of school.

**3** She _____ (will be) happier if she _____ (not work)
there, but she refuses to change jobs.

**4** Rohan _____ (will trust) you if you _____ (keep)
your promises, but you often breaks them.

**5** More people _____ (will eat) at that restaurant if the waiters
_____ (be) more polite. Unfortunately, they're very rude.

**C** 예시와 같이 주어진 문장을 If로 시작하는 가정법 문장으로 바꿔 쓰세요.

**0** I wanted to buy a laptop, but I didn't have the money.
→ If I had had the money, I would have bought a laptop.

**1** I wanted to have a pet, but I didn't have enough time to take care of one.
→ _____

**2** I wanted to read *Harry Potter* in English, but I wasn't good enough at English.
→ _____

**3** I want to have a talk with the German man, but I am not able to speak German.
→ _____

**D** 괄호 안에서 알맞은 것을 고르세요.

**1** If you (lose / lost) your health, you can't do what you want.
**2** If I (had /had had) a car, I would have driven to work.
**3** If I (am / were) president of Korea, I would reunite the two Koreas.
**4** If Jack (weren't / hadn't been) late for school, his teacher wouldn't have gotten angry with him.

---

## WRITING PRACTICE

우리말과 일치하도록 [보기]의 조동사와 괄호 안의 말을 이용하여 문장을 완성하세요.

[보기]  will      would

**1** 너희가 지금 집에서 떠난다면, 3시에 그곳에 도착할 거야. (leave, arrive)

If you _____ _____ now, you _____ _____ there at 3:00.

**2** 내가 중국어를 할 수 있다면, 내가 중국인 관광객들을 안내할 텐데. (be, guide)

If I _____ able to speak Chinese, I _____ _____ Chinese tourists.

**3** 내가 용기가 있었다면, 이 꽃들을 Floria에게 주었을 텐데. (be, give)

If I _____ _____ brave, I _____ _____ _____ these flowers to Floria.

# UNIT 52 다양한 형태의 가정법

정답 및 해설 p.80

## CHECK UP
괄호 안에서 알맞은 것을 고르세요.

**1** I wish I (am / were) the prince of Monaco. `A·1`

**2** I wish I (know / had known) it was Ann's birthday yesterday. `A·2`

**3** Linda spends money as if she (is / were) a millionaire; in fact, she's not. `B·1`

**4** It's time you (knew / will know) the truth. `C·1`

**5** If it (were not / had not been) for your help, I couldn't have passed the exam. `C·2`

## A
괄호 안의 동사를 알맞은 형태로 바꾸어 빈칸을 완성하세요.

**1** I wish I _____ (accept) my friend's advice at that time.

**2** I wish I _____ (am) a film director now.

**3** Jack dances as if he _____ (be) a professional dancer, but he's not.

**4** I wish I _____ (don't eat) ramyeon last night.

**5** It's time you _____ (stop) playing on the computer. It's already midnight.

## B
두 문장이 같은 뜻이 되도록 빈칸에 알맞은 말을 쓰세요.

**1** Without soccer, my life would be very boring.

= If _____, my life would be very boring.

**2** I wish I lived in Spain.

= I'm sorry _____.

**3** I wish I had read many good books when I was young.

= I'm sorry _____ when I was young.

**4** If it had not been for e-mail, I wouldn't have heard the news so soon.

= _____ e-mail, I wouldn't have heard the news so soon.

**130** G-ZONE WORKBOOK

**C** 괄호 안에서 알맞은 것을 고르세요.

**1** I (hope / wish) I can see you tomorrow morning.

**2** It's (high / right) time we left for the airport.

**3** (But for / Without for) your help, I would not have succeeded.

**4** I want to be alone. I wish I (didn't live / don't live) with my parents.

**5** I wish I (hadn't had to / didn't have to) study, but I have so much homework to do.


**D** 빈칸에 알맞은 말을 써서 주어진 문장에 담긴 실제 의미를 나타내는 문장을 완성하세요.

**1** Richard talks as if his father were a successful lawyer.

→ In fact, his father _____ _____ a successful lawyer.

**2** Tom and Bob spoke as though they knew each other.

→ In fact, they _____ _____ each other.

**3** Judy acted as if she had never met me before.

→ In fact, she _____ _____ me before.

**4** I wish I had gone to see a doctor when I first got sick.

→ I'm sorry I _____ _____ to see a doctor when I first got sick.


## WRITING PRACTICE

우리말과 일치하도록 괄호 안의 동사를 알맞은 형태로 바꾸어 문장을 완성하세요.

**1** 시간을 거꾸로 돌릴 수 있다면 좋을 텐데. (can turn back)

I _____ I _____ _____ _____ time.

**2** 그 책이 없었다면, 나는 기차에서 지루했을 텐데. (be)

If it _____ _____ _____ _____ the book, I _____ _____

_____ bored on the train.

**3** Mina는 Jina보다 더 어리지만 마치 Jina의 언니처럼 보인다. (look, be)

Mina is younger than Jina, but she _____ _____ _____ she _____

Jina's older sister.

↗ **CHECK UP**    괄호 안에서 알맞은 것을 고르세요.

**1** Every minute and second (is / are) precious to me.    `A-1`

**2** My son, as well as my daughters, (like / likes) dolls.    `A-2`

**3** Thirty minutes (is / are) a short time to take a nap.    `A-4`

**4** A quarter of my classmates (has / have) caught a cold.    `A-5`

**5** The number of homeless people (has / have) increased.    `A-5`

**A**    우리말과 일치하도록 괄호 안의 동사를 알맞은 형태로 바꾸어 빈칸을 완성하세요.

**1** 그 가게에는 많은 음반들이 있다.

There _____ (be) a number of records in the store.

**2** James도 그의 친구들도 잠들 수 없었다.

Neither James nor his friends _____ (be) able to sleep.

**3** 오늘 밤 TV에서 하는 쇼 프로그램들은 지루하다.

The shows on TV tonight _____ (be) boring.

**4** 10달러는 내 아버지에게는 많은 돈이 아니다.

Ten dollars _____ (be) not much money to my father.

**B**    문장의 밑줄 친 부분을 바르게 고쳐 쓰세요.

**1** Most of the police I met <u>was</u> very kind.    _____

**2** The total number of deaths <u>were</u> 945.    _____

**3** Three hours <u>are</u> a long time for a movie.    _____

**4** Most of the information <u>are</u> written in Spanish.    _____

**5** Not only my house but also those of my friends <u>was</u> damaged.    _____

**C**  주어진 문장을 과거시제로 바꾸어 다시 쓰세요.

**1** I guess Jacob will be going back to his parents' house.

→ I guessed that _____ .

**2** Kelly wants to say that she is sorry.

→ Kelly wanted to say that _____ .

**3** I think she has paid too much for the taxi from the airport to the city center.

→ I thought _____ .

**4** Jay says that he hurt his toe.

→ Jay said that _____ .

**D**  우리말과 일치하도록 괄호 안에서 알맞은 것을 모두 고르세요.

**1** Dan은 매일 아침 산책을 한다고 말했다.

Dan said that he (takes / took / had taken) a walk every morning.

**2** Harry는 그 파티에 올 수 없다고 말했다.

Henry said that he (wasn't able to / couldn't / can't have) come to the party.

**3** 내 남동생은 7 곱하기 2가 14라는 것을 알고 있었다.

My younger brother knew that seven times two (is / was / had been) fourteen.

## WRITING PRACTICE

우리말과 일치하도록 괄호 안의 말을 이용하여 문장을 완성하세요.

**1** 그 박물관에서 많은 그림들이 도난당했다. (number of painting)

_____ _____ _____ _____ _____ stolen from the museum.

**2** 사흘은 이 프로젝트를 끝내기에 충분한 시간이 아니다. (day, be)

_____ _____ _____ not enough time to finish this project.

**3** 자신의 웹페이지를 가진 학생들의 수가 늘고 있다. (number, be)

_____ _____ _____ students who have their own web pages _____

increasing.

**4** 나는 그 휴대전화가 내가 사기에 너무 비싸다고 생각했다. (think, be)

I _____ the cell phone _____ too expensive for me to buy.

# UNIT 54 화법

정답 및 해설 p.83

## ⤢ CHECK UP 괄호 안에서 알맞은 것을 고르세요.

**1** Joseph (said / told) that he wanted to go to Bali.  `A-2`

**2** Bob (said / told) me that he lost my umbrella.  `A-2`

**3** John asked what (are you / I was) doing.  `B-1`

**4** Bill asked Janis (do you like / if she liked) tulips.  `B-2`

**5** She told me not (shout / to shout).  `C`

## A 주어진 직접화법 문장을 간접화법 문장으로 바꿔 쓰세요.

**1** Kevin said, "I don't understand."

→ Kevin _____.

**2** The woman asked me, "What do you do for a living?"

→ The woman _____.

**3** My friend asked me, "Do you like him?"

→ My friend _____.

**4** The guard said to me, "Open your bag."

→ The guard _____.

**5** Lisa said to me, "Please don't tell anyone the secret."

→ Lisa _____.

## B 직접화법의 부사구를 간접화법에 맞게 바꿀 때, 빈칸에 알맞은 말을 쓰세요.

| 직접화법 | → | 간접화법 | 직접화법 | → | 간접화법 |
|---|---|---|---|---|---|
| this | → | that | yesterday | → | **1** _____ |
| now | → | **2** _____ | tomorrow | → | **3** _____ |
| here | → | **4** _____ | last year | → | the year before |
| ago | → | **5** _____ | next month | → | the following month |

**134**  G-ZONE WORKBOOK

**C** 직접화법을 간접화법으로 바꿀 때, 밑줄 친 부분을 바르게 고쳐 쓰세요.

**1** Jane said, "I will go to the concert on Friday."

→ Jane <u>told that I will go</u> to the concert on Friday.

_____

**2** I asked him, "Did you work last night?"

→ I asked him <u>if did he work</u> the night before.

_____

**3** Jessica said to me, "Please put this file on my desk."

→ Jessica <u>asked me if I put</u> that file on her desk.

_____

**D** 어법상 틀린 부분을 고쳐 문장을 다시 쓰세요.

**1** Tony asked that I was hurt.

→ _____

**2** She asked us we were happy or not.

→ _____

**3** He asked to me what I wanted to have for lunch.

→ _____

---

**WRITING PRACTICE**

우리말과 일치하도록 괄호 안의 말을 이용하여 직접화법 문장을 완성한 후, 간접화법 문장으로 바꿔 쓰세요.

**1** 엘비스 프레슬리는 "나는 음악에 대해서는 아무것도 모른다."고 말했다. (know, anything)

Elvis Presley _____, "_____ _____ _____ _____ about music."

→ Elvis Presley _____ _____ _____ _____ _____ about music.

**2** Kevin은 Suzy에게 "너 결혼했니?"라고 물었다. (be married)

Kevin _____ Suzy, "_____ _____ _____?"

→ Kevin _____ Suzy _____ _____ _____ _____.

**3** 종원은 나에게 "내일 부산행 첫 기차가 몇 시에 있니?"라고 물었다. (be)

Jongwon asked me, "_____ _____ the first train to Busan tomorrow?"

→ Jongwon asked me _____ _____ _____ _____ to Busan

_____ _____ _____ _____.

# UNIT 55 부정 표현, 부가의문문, 강조, 도치(So / Neither)

정답 및 해설 p.85

↗ **CHECK UP**  괄호 안에서 알맞은 것을 고르세요.

**1** I (can / can't) hardly believe what I'm looking at.  `A·2`

**2** It's Thursday, (is / isn't) it?  `B·1`

**3** I did (tell / told) you that you have to be more careful!  `C·1`

**4** It was in 1592 (that / what) the war broke out.  `C·2`

**5** A: I don't remember her face.  `D·2`
   B : (So / Neither) do I.

---

**A**  빈칸에 알맞은 부가의문문을 쓰세요.

**1** It's hot today, _____ _____?

**2** She doesn't like summer, _____ _____?

**3** He can cook Italian food, _____ _____?

**4** You remember Mark, _____ _____?

**5** I gained some weight, _____ _____?

---

**B**  밑줄 친 부분을 강조하는 문장으로 다시 쓰세요.

**1** Eddie broke his leg skiing.
   → It _____.

**2** They met by chance at a restaurant.
   → It _____.

**3** The Park family moved to Canada in 2003.
   → It _____.

**4** My friend started golf lessons yesterday.
   → It _____.

**5** Joey loves sandwiches and fresh salads.
   → Joey _____.

**6** He left the meeting without a word.
   → He _____.

**136**  G-ZONE WORKBOOK

**C**   괄호 안의 우리말과 일치하도록 so 또는 neither를 써서 B의 대답을 완성하세요.

**1** A: She is good at math.

B : _____. (나도 수학을 잘해.)

**2** A: I went to Berlin last year.

B : _____. (나도 작년에 베를린에 갔어.)

**3** A: Henry can't speak French.

B : _____. (나 역시 프랑스어를 못 해.)

**4** A: I won't forgive him.

B : _____. (나도 그를 용서하지 않을 거야.)


**D**   어법상 틀린 부분을 고쳐 문장을 다시 쓰세요.

**1** It's not very far, isn't it?

→ _____

**2** I have a few time to study.

→ _____

**3** We could not hardly see the stage.

→ _____

**4** I can't never understand her behavior.

→ _____


## WRITING PRACTICE

우리말과 일치하도록 괄호 안의 말을 바르게 배열하여 문장을 완성하세요.

**1** 오래 걸리지는 않겠죠, 그렇죠? (will, won't, it, long, take)

→ It _____?

**2** 내가 친구와 함께 캄보디아에 간 것은 작년이었다. (last year, went to, that, was, I, Cambodia)

→ It _____ with my friend.

**3** 나는 밖이 너무 시끄러워서 잠을 거의 못 잤다. (too, slept, it, was, because, noisy, hardly)

→ I _____ outside.

# 실전 TEST 06 Unit 51-55

**1** 다음 중 [보기]의 밑줄 친 부분과 같은 역할을 하는 것을 고르세요.

> [보기]  They think I don't know. But I <u>do</u> know.

① Will you <u>do</u> me a favor?
② <u>Do</u> you agree with me?
③ Mary <u>did</u> go to church yesterday.
④ Can you help me <u>do</u> the dishes?
⑤ Jack likes listening to music and so <u>do</u> I.

서술형

**2** 다음 빈칸에 들어갈 알맞은 말을 쓰세요.

> (1) Paul can drive and so _____ Sandra.
> (2) Jenny lives in New York and so _____ Jack.

**3** 다음 밑줄 친 부분 중 어법상 옳지 <u>않은</u> 것을 모두 고르세요. (2개)

① Two hours <u>is</u> enough. It will do.
② Not only I but also she <u>is</u> interested in learning Spanish.
③ Half of the coins <u>has</u> fallen to the ground.
④ Quality <u>counts for</u> more than quantity.
⑤ Neither they nor I <u>were</u> waiting for her when she got back.

서술형

**[4-5]** 다음 문장을 간접화법 문장으로 바꿔 쓰세요.

**4**
> She always says to me, "Clean your room."

→ She always _____ me _____ _____ _____ room.

**5**
> Norah asked me, "What do you have in your bag?"

→ Norah _____ _____ _____ _____ _____ in _____ bag.

**6** 다음 중 문장의 의미를 해석한 것이 옳지 <u>않은</u> 것을 고르세요.

① If it had not been for his care, I would have been in the hospital longer.
  → Without his care, I would have been in the hospital longer.
② I will call you if I have questions.
  → I may have questions. I will call you if I do.
③ If it were not raining, we could go on a picnic.
  → It is raining, so we can't go on a picnic.
④ It is time I made dinner for my children.
  → I just finished making dinner for my children.
⑤ Adel talks as if she had performed better than Kieun.
  → In fact, Adel didn't perform better than Kieun.

**7** 다음 우리말과 일치하도록 빈칸에 들어갈 말이 바르게 짝 지어진 것을 고르세요.

> • 모든 거주자가 떠난 것은 아니지만, 아주 소수의 사람만 현재 거기에 살고 있다.
> → _____ of the residents are gone, but very few people live there now.
> • 너는 한국에 곧 돌아올 거야, 그렇지?
> → You will come back to Korea very soon, _____ you?
> • Josh는 그의 경험에서 귀중한 교훈을 배웠다.
> → Josh _____ learn a valuable lesson from his experience.

① None - won't - did
② None - will - does
③ Not all - won't - do
④ Not all - will - did
⑤ Not all - won't - did

**8** 다음 중 우리말 해석이 <u>어색한</u> 것을 고르세요.

① All that glitters is not gold.
   → 반짝이는 모든 것이 금은 아니다.
② Can you speak up? I can hardly hear you.
   → 크게 말해줄래? 네 말을 열심히 들을 수 있어.
③ I want to have either a car or a motorcycle.
   → 나는 차나 오토바이 둘 중 하나를 가지고 싶다.
④ I thought she would call me straight away.
   → 나는 그녀가 내게 즉시 전화할 것이라고 생각했다.
⑤ You stayed there for a while, didn't you?
   → 너 거기에서 잠시 머물렀지, 그렇지 않니?

**9** 다음 중 빈칸에 들어갈 부가의문문이 바르게 짝지어진 것을 고르세요.

> • She likes going shopping, _____?
> • We did not talk about it, _____?
> • Ted doesn't eat meat, _____?

① doesn't she - did we - does he
② does she - didn't we - does Ted
③ doesn't she - did we - doesn't Ted
④ does she - didn't we - does he
⑤ doesn't she - didn't we - does Ted

**10** 다음 중 화법 전환이 바르게 되지 <u>않은</u> 것을 고르세요.

① He told her to come and help him.
   → He said to her, "Come and help me."
② I asked him how he could play golf so well.
   → I asked him, "How can you play golf so well?"
③ He said that his son was the biggest joy in his life.
   → He said, "My son is the biggest joy in my life."
④ I asked Billy what he was going to do.
   → I asked Billy, "What are you going to do?"
⑤ He told me that he looked forward to seeing my game.
   → He said to me, "I look forward to seeing my game."

**11** 다음 [보기]에서 알맞은 말을 골라 빈칸을 채우세요.

[보기]  every   few   none   hardly

(1) _____ people participated in the project, so it took long time to finish it.

(2) She _____ eats anything, so she looks like a skeleton these days.

**[12-13]** 다음 중 어법상 옳지 않은 것을 고르세요.

**12** ① I wish I didn't wear glasses.
② If he were here right now, he could help us.
③ If she did more exercise, she would be healthier.
④ If you had come to the party, I would have been happy.
⑤ I wish I know there were more tickets left.

**13** ① He does consume too much sugar.
② It was Sophie who passed the final interview.
③ It was across the street on Kennedy Avenue that Chen found her old classmate.
④ He asked me whether I had any plans for Saturday.
⑤ I couldn't hardly hear what he said.

**[14-16]** 다음 우리말과 일치하도록 괄호 안의 말을 알맞은 형태로 바꾸어 문장을 완성하세요.

**14** 나는 내가 예술가면 좋겠어!
(wish, be, an artist)

→ _____

_____!

**15** 내가 내 친구의 조언을 듣지 않았더라면 좋을 텐데. 그러면 나는 그림 그리는 것을 더 일찍 시작했을 텐데! (wish, not listen to, my friend's advice)

→ _____

_____.

Then I'd have started painting earlier!

**16** 내가 봉급을 저축했더라면 나는 그 집을 구입할 수 있었을 텐데. (save, my salary, can, buy)

→ If I _____

_____ the house.

**17** 다음 밑줄 친 부분의 해석이 옳지 않은 것을 고르세요.

① When you'd like to order, please press the buzzer. → 주문하고 싶으시면
② I wouldn't believe him if he looked suspicious. → 그 남자가 수상해 보인다면
③ He asked me if Susan would come over. → 수잔이 온다면
④ If I had known the concert was canceled, I wouldn't have gone there. → 그 콘서트가 취소된 것을 알았더라면
⑤ If it wasn't raining so much, we could go out for a walk. → 비가 아주 많이 오지 않는다면

**18** 다음 중 화법 전환이 바르게 된 것을 고르세요.

① He said to me, "I am tired."
→ He asked me that he is tired.
② They asked me, "Can you speak Korean?"
→ They asked me if I can speak Korean.
③ He said to me, "I am proud of you."
→ He told me that he was proud of me.
④ She asked me, "What do you want?"
→ She asked me what she wanted.
⑤ He said to me, "I will wait for you."
→ He told me if he would wait for me.

**19** 다음 중 밑줄 친 문장을 과거시제로 바르게 전환한 것을 고르세요.

Marco Polo remembers all he has seen and heard, and had it written down in a book. People, however, did not believe his story to be true for a long time. They could not think it was possible that there were such great and rich countries like China and India, with millions and millions of people. And the silk, jewels, delicious foods, and sweet scents about which he talked seemed untrue.

① Marco Polo remembered all he sees and hears
② Marco Polo remembered all he have seen and heard
③ Marco Polo remembered all he has seen and heard
④ Marco Polo remembered all he had seen and heard
⑤ Marco Polo remembered all he saw and has heard

서술형

**[20-21]** 다음 글을 읽고, 물음에 답하세요.

ⓐ Castles are beautiful, aren't it? They look amazing with their towers and *drawbridges. But ⓑ few castles were built just to look pretty! Old stone castles were strong fortresses. ⓒ It is said that castles had high towers so archers could easily fight off attackers. (A) Moats protected castles, too! A moat is a *ditch that goes around a castle. Moats were often filled with water. If a castle had a moat, ⓓ attackers would be in serious trouble! Thanks to such barriers, there are even some castles that ⓔ have never been defeated.

*drawbridge 도개교(들어올릴 수 있는 다리)
*ditch (들판·도로가의) 배수로

**20** ⓐ~ⓔ에서 어법상 옳지 않은 것의 기호를 쓰고 틀린 부분을 바르게 고쳐 쓰세요.

_____ → _____

**21** 밑줄 친 문장 (A)를 동사를 강조한 문장으로 다시 쓰세요.

→ _____

_____

**MEMO**

## 지은이

### NE능률 영어교육연구소

NE능률 영어교육연구소는 혁신적이며 효율적인 영어 교재를 개발하고
영어 학습의 질을 한 단계 높이고자 노력하는 NE능률의 연구조직입니다.

# GRAMMAR ZONE WORKBOOK 〈기초편〉

펴 낸 이   주민홍
펴 낸 곳   서울특별시 마포구 월드컵북로 396(상암동) 누리꿈스퀘어 비즈니스타워 10층
          (주)NE능률 (우편번호 03925)
펴 낸 날   2017년 1월 5일 개정판 제1쇄
          2023년 12월 15일 제17쇄
전   화   02 2014 7114
팩   스   02 3142 0356
홈페이지   www.neungyule.com
등록번호   제 1-68호
I S B N   979-11-253-1236-9  53740
정   가   8,000원

NE 능률

## 고객센터

교재 내용 문의 : contact.nebooks.co.kr (별도의 가입 절차 없이 작성 가능)
제품 구매, 교환, 불량, 반품 문의 : 02-2014-7114
☎ 전화문의는 본사 업무시간 중에만 가능합니다.

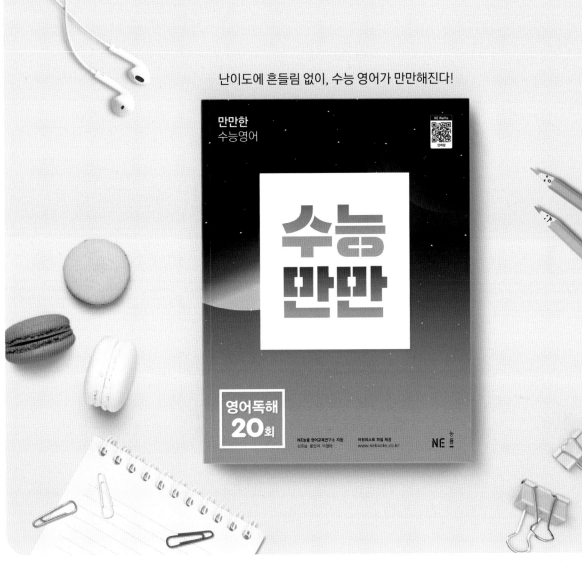